2 JOHN
3 JOHN
and
JUDE

J. Vernon McGee

THOMAS NELSON PUBLISHERS

Nashville

Published in Nashville, Tennessee, by Thomas Nelson, Inc., and distributed in Canada by Lawson Falle, Ltd., Cambridge, Ontario.

Quotations from *Word Studies in the Greek New Testament* (Jude) by Kenneth S. Wuest. William B. Eerdmans Publishing Company. Used by permission.

Scripture quotations are from the KING JAMES VERSION of the Bible.

Library of Congress Cataloging-in-Publication Data

McGee, J. Vernon (John Vernon), 1904–1988
   [Thru the Bible with J. Vernon McGee]
   Thru the Bible commentary series / J. Vernon McGee.
     p.   cm.
   Reprint. Originally published: Thru the Bible with J. Vernon McGee. 1975.
   Includes bibliographical references.
   ISBN 0-8407-3310-0
   1. Bible—Commentaries. I. Title.
BS491.2.M37 1991
220.7'7—dc20   90–41340
                                          CIP

Printed in the United States of America

1 2 3 4 5 6 7 — 96 95 94 93 92 91

CONTENTS

2 JOHN

2 JOHN

JUDE

PREFACE

The radio broadcasts of the Thru the Bible Radio five-year program were transcribed, edited, and published first in single-volume paperbacks to accommodate the radio audience.

There has been a minimal amount of further editing for this publication. Therefore, these messages are not the word-for-word recording of the taped messages which went out over the air. The changes were necessary to accommodate a reading audience rather than a listening audience.

These are popular messages, prepared originally for a radio audience. They should not be considered a commentary on the entire Bible in any sense of that term. These messages are devoid of any attempt to present a theological or technical commentary on the Bible. Behind these messages is a great deal of research and study in order to interpret the Bible from a popular rather than from a scholarly (and too-often boring) viewpoint.

We have definitely and deliberately attempted "to put the cookies on the bottom shelf so that the kiddies could get them."

The fact that these messages have been translated into many languages for radio broadcasting and have been received with enthusiasm reveals the need for a simple teaching of the whole Bible for the masses of the world.

I am indebted to many people and to many sources for bringing this volume into existence. I should express my especial thanks to my secretary, Gertrude Cutler, who supervised the editorial work; to Dr. Elliott R. Cole, my associate, who handled all the detailed work with the publishers; and finally, to my wife Ruth for tenaciously encouraging me from the beginning to put my notes and messages into printed form.

Solomon wrote, ". . . of making many books there is no end; and much study is a weariness of the flesh" (Eccl. 12:12). On a sea of books that flood the marketplace, we launch this series of THRU THE BIBLE with the hope that it might draw many to the one Book, *The Bible*.

J. VERNON MCGEE

2 JOHN

The Second Epistle of

JOHN

INTRODUCTION

A man whom I knew years ago in the South had the best way to divide the three epistles of John that I have ever heard. He called them "one-eyed John," "two-eyed John," and "three-eyed John." I do not think you will forget the three epistles of John if you remember them like this. That man, by the way, was one of the three conservative ministers in the community in which I served in Nashville, Tennessee, at that time. He was a real brother in Christ. Any Christian, regardless of his race, nationality, or station in life, if he is right on the inside, if he has been born again, is my brother. That is the great truth taught in 1 John which will be continued in 2 and 3 John with a different emphasis.

We are considering here, then, "two-eyed John." Your first impression, I am sure, is the brevity of these two last epistles. It is something that is almost startling. You might wonder why just thirteen verses in the second epistle and fourteen verses in the third epistle should be included in the Scriptures. Both of the epistles are very brief indeed. Someone will say, "Doesn't their brevity discount their message? Obviously, John didn't have too much to say." Not at all. Their brevity does not in any way take away from the importance of these epistles. In fact, it actually enhances them. Although they are very brief, these epistles are very important, and they are essential for getting a proper perspective of the first epistle and avoiding a perverted viewpoint. Let me illustrate it like this. My doctor at one time gave me two kinds of medication that I was to take whenever I suffered certain symptoms.

One was a pill so small that I had trouble locating it in the bottle. The other was a capsule which looked like it was too big to swallow. I needed almost a gallon of water to get it down—I had to float it first! But I discovered in using both of them that the smaller one, the teeny-weeny one, was the more potent of the two. In fact, I found out it was the more important one: if the big one didn't work, then I used the little one. So it is with 2 and 3 John. Their brevity does not make them less potent.

The writer of this epistle is the apostle John. We call him the apostle of love. The Lord Jesus called him a "son of thunder" (see Mark 3:17). I think you can add to the thunder a little lightning, for in his epistles he makes it very clear that you must exhibit love to the brethren or you are not a child of God. John wrote this epistle around A.D. 90–100.

This epistle is like the Book of Philemon in that it is a personal letter. It is written by John to "the elect lady." The question is often asked whether the Greek word *electa* is a title or whether it refers to a Christian lady in the early church by the name of Electa. You must recall that John is the apostle who writes of the family of God. Paul writes of the church of God, while Peter writes of the government of God. If you will keep that in the background of your thinking as you come to these epistles written by these different men, it will help you understand many things they are saying. Regardless of whether it is addressed to an individual or to a church, John is thinking of it in the context of the family of God. Apparently, there was some Christian lady or a local church which was extending hospitality to all those who claimed to be Christian, although some were heretics who denied the deity of Christ and the other great truths of the Christian faith. John warns here in this epistle against entertaining such folk. This is actually the purpose of this little epistle.

The theme of this epistle is: "For truth's sake." When truth and love come into conflict, truth is the one that is to predominate; it is the one that has top priority. Have you noticed that in 1 Corinthians 13:13 Paul didn't say, "Now abideth faith, hope, truth, and love"? He just said, "And now abideth faith, hope, charity [love], these three; but the greatest of these is charity [love]." But when truth is brought in, then truth comes first.

In other words, truth is worth contending for, and it is wrong to receive false teachers. This is the position that I take very definitely. I believe that the truth in the Word of God is worth contending for. When I say truth, I mean, first, that which is basic to the fact that the Bible is the Word of God—there is no question in my mind about it. The second thing of essential importance is the deity of Christ and His work upon the cross for us. When I meet a man who is true on these essentials, then he and I can disagree on nonessentials. I have a very good friend who is a Pentecostal preacher. When we play golf, he and I naturally get into a friendly argument. I always end up by saying to him, "Brother, you and I agree on so many things. I love to hear you talk about the Lord Jesus and about His death on the cross. You thrill my heart when I hear you talk about those things. But I want you to know that we disagree on a few points, and I'm going to pray for you because I think you are wrong." Well, you know he turns around and says the same thing to me, and we leave each other laughing. As far as I know, that man has never said an unkind word to me or about me. He is my brother. I wish he could see some things as I do, but it will just have to be that way until he gets a little more light—and I want to be patient with him! But he stands true on the inspiration of the Scriptures, he stands true on the deity of Christ, and he stands true on the fact that Christ died for us. When a man does that, he's my brother, and I cannot escape that fact.

The key word in John's first epistle is love, but it is a love that is confined to the family of God. The little children are to love each other in the family of God. This is the mark of a child of God: he loves Christ, and he loves the brethren. How God's little children are to love each other is the entire sum and substance of that epistle.

It would be helpful to go back to the first epistle and pick up this thought again: "In this the children of God are manifest, and the children of the devil: whosoever doeth not righteousness is not of God, neither he that loveth not his brother" (1 John 3:10). John purposely cast this truth in the negative so that there would be no way in the world that any individual who claims to be a Christian and does not measure up could wiggle out of it. You cannot wiggle out of this: if you do not practice righteousness in your life, you are not of God. This is the outward badge of a child of God. You are to know the Lord Jesus as your Savior, and the proof to others is that you practice righteousness in your life. And if you do not love your brother (your Christian brother—this is not the universal brotherhood of man, for the Bible does not teach that), then you are not a child of God. I didn't say this—John said it. If you don't like it, then you take it up with him. John said that you can tell if someone is a genuine believer by his righteous life and his love for other Christians.

But what about the lost sinner who is not in the family of God? Are we to love him? Well, we are told in the Gospel of John: "For God so loved the world, that he gave his only begotten Son, that whosoever believeth in him should not perish, but have everlasting life" (John 3:16). Follow me carefully now. We are to love people to the extent of taking the Gospel to them. We see in the Book of Jonah that Jonah did not love the Ninevites, but God sent him there because God loved them and God said, "Since I love them and they have turned to Me, Jonah, I want you to love them also." This is the relationship the child of God is to have to the lost world. You cannot love the sinners and their sin—we are not asked to do that. We are asked to love them enough to take the Gospel to them. That is the important thing. We are to love them in that sense because God loves them. And then, when they turn to Christ, we will love them also.

Now another question arises: What is to be our relationship to false teachers, to those who deny the deity of Christ? John is going to make it very clear in this second epistle that this is something we need to beware of. He says in verse 7, "For many deceivers are entered into the world, who confess not that Jesus Christ is come in the flesh. This is a deceiver and an antichrist." What should be our relationship to false teachers? Follow me very carefully because this is going to be the nub of this epistle, and if you and I don't get this correctly, we are going to go haywire in our interpretation and come up with a pseudo liberal viewpoint. All of this "love, love, love" stuff today actually is not biblical at all. We are told to love everybody, but there are some whom the

Scriptures tell us not to love but to be very careful of. John writes, "Love not the world, neither the things that are in the world . . ." (1 John 2:15). The things that are in the world are identified with the people who are in the world and who have made it as it is. Our love is to take the Gospel to them, to give them the Word of God.

John's emphasis in his first epistle is upon love, but the key word in this second epistle is truth. Now when truth and love are in contrast and conflict, which one should prevail? If we get the answer to that, then that will determine our relationship to the false teacher, to the one who denies the deity of Christ. The so-called apostle of love is going to shock you and me out of our sentimental complacency and our sloppy notion of love. Which one should prevail—truth or love? His startling reply is that *truth* comes first. Christ said, "I am the way, the truth, and the life." He didn't say, "I am love," but He said, ". . . I am the way, the truth, and the life: no man cometh unto the Father, but by me" (John 14:6). You have to come to the Father through Jesus Christ. There is no other way. Why? Because He's not only the Way, but He is the truth. It was John who wrote later on that "God is love." After the Lord Jesus was here and had said that He was the truth, then John said, "God is love" (see 1 John 4:16). My friend, love can be expressed only within the bounds and context of truth. Love can be expressed only within the limitation and boundary that Scripture sets. Therefore, what about the false teacher? May I say to you, you are not to love the false teacher. John is going to make that abundantly clear. In fact, he is going to say something quite amazing. He says, "You are not even to entertain him in your home. You are not in any way to receive him or to have fellowship with him." That is just about as strong as it possibly can be.

We need to notice another important word in order to get a proper perspective of what John will be talking about in this second epistle as well as in the third epistle. In the first epistle John said that we are to ". . . walk in the light, as he is in the light . . ." (1 John 1:7). Truth and light are the same; they are the Word of God. As we have already seen, love and truth are inseparable. Christ is the epitome of both; He is the incarnation of both. He is *the* truth, and He is love. God is love, and He is God. In addition to *truth*, there is a second word which is featured in this brief epistle—it is the word *walk*. In 2 John 4 you will notice that John says, "I rejoiced greatly that I found of thy children *walking* in truth, as we have received a commandment from the Father" (italics mine). And then in 2 John 6, we read, "And this is love, that we *walk* after his commandments. This is the commandment, That, as ye have heard from the beginning, ye should *walk* in it" (italics mine). Back in the first epistle, John wrote, "In this the children of God are manifest, and the children of the devil: whosoever doeth not righteousness is not of God, neither he that loveth not his brother" (1 John 3:10). That righteousness is Christ, and to deny the deity of Christ is certainly not to do righteousness—the truth is essential. "Neither he that loveth not his brother"—this is the second thing that is very important, the walk. With this second word, we go to the opposite end of the spectrum of the Christian life. Not only is truth essential, but the walk is essential, and therefore we are told to love the brethren.

This epistle, therefore, will not give us a balanced viewpoint of the first epistle. Our contemporary idea of "love, love, love," that we are to love everyone who comes along, I do not find in the Word of God. When John is speaking of love here, he makes it clear that it is love within the family of God. We need to be very careful about this because a great many are interpreting *agape* love as nothing in the world but sex. One morning I received a phone call from a lady who had come to know the Lord through our radio ministry. She said to me, "Dr. McGee, I just want you to know that I love you." She sort of caught herself and then said, "I hope you understand that I'm not talking about man and woman love. I'm saying that I love you as a brother in the Lord who led me to Christ." Well, I understand that, and I believe that is the kind of love which John is talking about here.

This love in the family of God needs to be exhibited today in the church. I think it is time for many of the churches that have built up a reputation for being fundamental in the faith to now exhibit love among the brethren. I would say that I need that in my own life; I am sure you need more love in your life also.

However, this love is not to slop over. We need to recognize that it has a boundary within the family of God. Along comes one of these heretics, as they did in John's day. He is apostate; he is actually an antichrist; that is, he denies the deity of Christ. John says, "When one of these fellows comes along you are not to extend love to him. You are not even to entertain him."

OUTLINE

2 JOHN

The message of John's second epistle is essential to having a proper perspective of what he has said in his first epistle. He deals here with the polarity of the Christian life-truth and love. He answers the question: When truth and love come into conflict, which is to predominate, which is to have top priority?

LOVE EXPRESSED IN THE BOUNDARY OF TRUTH

The elder unto the elect lady and her children, whom I love in the truth; and not I only, but also all they that have known the truth [2 John 1].

The Second Epistle of John is a personal letter from "the elder unto the elect lady and her children." The Greek word for "elder" is *presbuteros* (presbyter), and it has a twofold meaning. It can mean a senior citizen, referring to age, or it can be a title, referring to an office in the church, a minister or a teacher. I am sure that John is primarily calling himself an elder, speaking of his office in the church. I think he also infers the fact that he is now an old man. He is actually up in his nineties, approaching one hundred, as he writes this epistle. Notice that John does not call upon his office as an apostle. I think the reason is quite obvious: the one to whom he is writing accepts his authority. All he calls himself here is "the elder."

"Unto the elect lady and her children." The word *electa* could be the name of a prominent woman in the church, or it could be the local church itself that John has in mind. "Her children" could be either the physical children of the woman or the spiritual children of the church. These could be interpreted either way. I emphasize the church rather than the individual, applying it to the church at large and the church today. When I say the church, I am not thinking of any local church or any denomination, but the total body of believers in the Lord Jesus Christ. This epistle has been relevant for the church down through the centuries, and what is written here has been very productive in the life of the church. I believe that since our contemporary church has such an emphasis on love, we need this little epistle to cause us to shape up and to get a correct perspective of what love is.

"Whom I love in the truth." The word truth is emphasized in this epistle, and as I have said in the introduction, it is the key word to the epistle. Christian love can only be expressed in the bounds of the family of God, those who have the truth. "The truth" here is the Word of God and also the One who is revealed in the Word, the Lord Jesus Christ Himself. "Whom I love in truth" is the correct, literal translation. John is saying two things here: (1) That the object of his love must be another believer in Christ, a genuine believer; and also (2) that he is genuine in asserting this, that expressing his love is not just a pious platitude he is uttering here.

"And not I only but also all they that have known the truth." John embraces the rest of the body of believers here. They also love either this church or this particular woman in the church because of her outstanding testimony.

For the truth's sake, which dwelleth in us, and shall be with us for ever [2 John 2].

"For the truth's sake" means a defense of the truth. We need to recognize that the truth needs to be defended. We need to stand for the truth of God and for the Word of God. Many of our so-called conservative men have adopted a very sophisticated and blasé method in an attempt to be clever in what they teach and preach. They will not come out flatfooted and say it just as it is, but they toy around with it and build up some clever alliteration. I'm for alliteration, as you well know, but the point is that the truth needs to be stated clearly.

I had an interesting encounter with a certain teacher several years ago. I was told by a student of his that he didn't believe a certain doctrine, and I quoted him on it. The man became very much irritated with me, which he had a right to be if I were wrong. I told him, "I'd like for you to clarify this. If you will just write me a letter and state clearly what you believe, I'll be very happy to read it and to make my apology." Instead of writing that kind of letter, he wrote a letter in which he made it clear he was highly incensed at me for even suggesting he didn't believe such and such a doctrine. So I wrote to him again and said, "All you have to do to clear this up is just to state clearly what you do believe." At the bottom of the page I wrote, "I believe———" and "I do not believe———" and I left him space for his answer, making it very easy for him to reply. That really irritated him, and I was blasted with another letter. So I dropped the matter and found out later that the reason he didn't answer was because he actually did not believe the doctrine I had questioned him about. But he had attempted to cover up his disbelief. My feeling is that I would respect him for what he believes. Although it is different from what I believe, I would never consider a man to be a heretic or an apostate who believes what he believes. But I cannot respect the fact that his method was and is today never to be clear on exactly what he does believe.

"For the truth's sake, which dwelleth in us, and shall be with us for ever." Thank God, we will have the truth forever. In this day when you can't believe politicians, you can't believe college professors, you can't believe the scientists, and you can't believe the military leadership, it's nice to have someone in whom you can believe—the Lord Jesus Christ. "For the truth's sake, which dwelleth in us"—the indwelling Spirit of God makes these things real to us. "And shall be with us for ever"—the truth will not change; it is unchangeable. Someone has put it like this: "What is true is not new, and what is new is not true." Like a great many generalizations, that has some exceptions to it, of course, but usually it is true.

In verse 3 John adopts a greeting that is a little different from that of Paul and Peter and James and even himself.

Grace be with you, mercy, and peace, from God the Father, and from the Lord Jesus Christ, the Son of the Father, in truth and love [2 John 3].

There are three words here that we need to be clear on in our thinking. They differ without there really being a great difference in the sense that they all apply to the same thing. The words are *love, mercy,* and *grace.* John introduces the word *mercy* here in his greeting.

What is the difference between the love, the mercy, and the grace of God? We read in Ephesians 2:4–5, "But God, who is rich in mercy, for his great love wherewith he loved us, Even when we were dead in sins, hath quickened us together with Christ, (by grace ye are saved;)." This is such a wonderful Scripture because it combines all three: Paul says that God is rich in *mercy,* and because of His great *love* for us, He saves us by *grace.* What is the love of God? Well, God is love. Before anything was created, God was love. Somebody says, "Whom did He love?" Well, the Trinity existed, and we know the love which existed between God the Father and God the Son. Dr. Lewis Sperry Chafer writes, "Love is that in God which existed before He would care to exercise mercy or grace." Love is the nature of God; it is what is called an attribute of God. God is love, but the interesting thing is that the love of God never saved a sinner. The love of God caused God to move in the direction of mercy and grace; it caused Him to exercise mercy and grace.

Now the question arises: What is the difference between mercy and grace? Dr. Chafer very exactly expresses it: "Mercy, on the other hand, is that in God which duly provided for the need of sinful man." God is rich in mercy. Why is He rich in mercy? Because He is love. And because God is love, He, by mercy, provided for the need of sinful man. But mercy didn't save man. Again, I quote Dr. Chafer: "Grace is that in Him which acts freely to save because all the demands of holiness have been satisfied." God today is free to act in grace. You are a sinner who cannot provide anything for God. You haven't anything to offer to Him. But now grace means that God can come to you, a lost sinner, and say, "I am love, and I am rich in mercy. I love you, and I have provided by My mercy a Savior for you." Now if you will trust Him, "By grace are ye saved through faith; and that not of yourselves: it is the gift of God" (Eph. 2:8).

There is a fine distinction here between these words, and someone will say, "It looks like a distinction without a difference." Well, there is a difference in that which doesn't differ. Salvation all stems from the love of God, but God does not save by His love or His mercy. After all, our God is a holy God, and the Bible says, "For God so loved the world, that he gave his only begotten Son . . ." (John 3:16). You see, God did not so love the world that He saved the world—He didn't do that. God so loved the world that by His mercy He provided a Savior for the world, and He can now save by grace.

There is something else here that is important to see. Salvation is not only the expression of the love of God, but it is also an expression of the justice and righteousness of God. We not only need John 3:16, but we also need Romans 3:26: "To declare, I say, at this time his righteousness: that he might be just, and the justifier of him which believeth in Jesus." In order to justify you when you trust Christ, God has to be righteous and holy and just. He cannot simply open the back door of heaven and slip you in under cover of darkness. You and I are not fit for heaven. We are alienated from Him. We have no fellowship with Him. Communication broke down in the Garden of Eden, and He is the one who renewed it. Because He must be just and righteous, His mercy provided a Savior, and it was because He loves you. He can be righteous and do this—"that he might be just, and the justifier of him which believeth in Jesus."

Therefore, John can now write, "Grace be with you"—that is the way God saves you. "Mercy"—mercy provided a Savior. "And peace"—when you have all this, then the peace of God that passeth all understanding is going to keep your heart. As John said, For the truth's sake, which dwelleth in us, and shall be with us forever." You will know that these great truths are not something which God is going to change. He is not going to change His mind tomorrow and say, "Well, I'm going to act differently. I think public opinion is going in another direction, so I'll change and go with public opinion." God doesn't change; He is not a weather vane. I am reminded of the farmer who had on his barn a weather vane which said on it, "God is love." A preacher drove up to the farm and said to this man, "Do you mean that God's love is as variable as that weather vane?" The farmer said, "No I don't mean that. I mean that it does not matter which way the wind is blowing, God is still love." My friend, that is true. Our God is love, and because He is love, He has provided salvation for you. He will never change.

"Grace be with you, mercy, and peace, from God the Father, and from the Lord Jesus Christ." The Lord Jesus Christ is the One who died for you. He is "the Son of the Father"—that is His position in the Trinity.

"In truth and love." Remember that love must be exercised in the context of truth. There are folk who write to me and say, "You are very dogmatic in your teaching." I always appreciate those letters because I am not always sure that I give that impression. I *want* to give that impression when I am teaching the Word of God. I am very dogmatic about it. Now if you ask me what I think I'll be doing this afternoon, I must say that I don't know because my wife hasn't decided yet! I'm not dogmatic about what I am going to do this afternoon. But right now I am writing about 2 John, and I am very dogmatic about what he says here.

I rejoiced greatly that I found of thy children walking in truth, as we have received a commandment from the Father [2 John 4].

"Thy children" are either the physical children of this woman or the members of the local church. I think it could be either, and it probably refers to both. "I rejoiced greatly that I found of thy children walking in truth." "Walking in truth" refers to the manner of life, meaning walking in obedience to the commandments from the Father. It is wonderful to have children who are walking in truth.

"As we have received a commandment from the Father." The commandment is that we walk in the light as He is in the light, that we order our lives by the Word of God.

And now I beseech thee, lady, not as though I wrote a new commandment unto thee, but that which we had from the beginning, that we love one another [2 John 5].

"The beginning" refers to the beginning of the ministry of Christ in His incarnation.

The teaching that the Lord Jesus gave was: "If ye love me, keep my commandments" (John 14:15). He said, "By this shall all men know that ye are my disciples"—not because you are fundamentalists but "if ye have love one to another" (John 13:35, italics mine). John says that this is the commandment that we have had from the beginning, that we are to love one another.

Here we have it: walking in truth and loving one another (again, we are talking about loving fellow believers). This is the balance that is needed today in the church, or else any church will become lopsided. We can become oversentimental in the church. There is a lot of sentimental tommyrot going on, and it is as sloppy as can be: "Oh, we love each other. We have the *agape* love"—and all that sort of thing. But are you walking in the truth? Are you really walking in the knowledge of the Word of God? All the apostles emphasized that we are to walk in love. My friend, this is very important in these days in which we live. It's wonderful if you are a fundamentalist—I hope you are—but I hope you are walking in love because you really are not a fundamentalist unless you are.

The objective polarity of the Christian faith and the Christian life is truth and love. John emphasized love in his first epistle, but he also said that that love is for the brethren, it is for believers, it is for those who are in Christ. He said, "My little children, I want you to love one another"—that is, other believers. I do not quite understand this idea of watering down the Christian faith and saying that we are to love everybody, because I know that when you make a statement like that, you don't love everybody. It is just impossible to do that. There are too many in this world who are unlovely. A lot of us are unlovely, and, as a result, we are not loved. But God loves the world. We are not worth loving, but God loves us all. The important thing is that He tells believers to take the Gospel to the world. *That* is the way that you and I can show our concern and love, if you want to call it that. We are to take the Gospel to the lost because God loves them, and then if we take it to them, a love will be begotten in our hearts for those who are actually our enemies. The important thing to see is that God is love—it is His attribute—and His love has provided a Savior for us. But truth is also very important, and you cannot put love above truth, because when

you do, then you sacrifce truth. This is John's emphasis in this second
epistle.

**And this is love, that we walk after his commandments.
This is the commandment, That, as ye have heard from
the beginning, ye should walk in it [2 John 6].**

What is love? It is to walk after His commandments. The Lord said, "If
ye love me, keep my commandments" (John 14:15). This is another
way of saying the same thing. The Lord's commandments are more
than the Ten Commandments. The Ten Commandments are basic to
government and basic to civilization, but the Christian is called to
a higher plane where he is to produce in his life, by the Spirit (it is
the fruit of the Spirit), love, joy, peace, longsuffering, etc. If these
things are in us and abide in us, you and I are walking after His commandments. If they are not in us, we are not walking after His
commandments.

"And this is love." Let me say it again: Love is not made in the
parlor—it is made in the kitchen. Love is not made in the bedroom—it
is made out there in the laundry room. Does she wash his clothes?
Does he bring home his paycheck? Does he support his family? That is
the way you express love in the family, and that is the way you express
love in the church—in your concern and in your help for others. You
cannot say that you are loving someone unless you have a concern for
him, especially a concern for his spiritual welfare.

"And this is love, that we walk after his commandments." Now this
is getting right down into shoe leather. This is getting right down
where the rubber meets the road. This is sidewalk salvation. It is that
which can walk down the street. You must recall that men like John
and Paul were writing to people who lived in the Roman world. In
Paul's day the emperor was bloody Nero. John saw one emperor after
another rise who persecuted the Christians. Beginning with Titus, the
Roman general who destroyed Jerusalem in A.D. 70, the persecution
was severe. The Roman world was a brutal world, a cruel world, a
world that was pagan to the core. And yet here were men and women
who were walking down Roman roads, living in pagan cities, and they

were walking after His commandments. They were translating the Gospel into life. This is the thing that is desperately needed in our day.

"This is the commandment, That as ye have heard from the beginning, ye should walk in it." In other words, John is saying, "This thing is not to be put on ice. It is not something to be stored on the shelf. You have heard it from the beginning. The Lord Jesus taught this. Now let's get busy and walk in it. Let's manifest love to those outside."

LIFE IS AN EXPRESSION OF THE
DOCTRINE OF CHRIST

Again there arises before us the other end of this polarization: love is on one side, and the truth is on the other. John now issues his warning—

> For many deceivers are entered into the world, who confess not that Jesus Christ is come in the flesh. This is a deceiver and an antichrist [2 John 7].

"An antichrist" should read the antichrist. John said in his first epistle that already there were many antichrists and that there was the spirit of antichrist. How do we identify the spirit of antichrist? John gives us the answer: "Who confess not that Jesus Christ is come in the flesh." The spirit of antichrist is to deny the deity of Christ. It is to deny everything that is said about Him, everything that He said, and everything that He did for us in redemption by dying on the cross and by being raised bodily from the dead. That is antichrist, and that is the spirit of antichrist.

The spirit of antichrist eventually will be headed up, I believe, not by one man but by two men, because two men are described in Revelation 13. One of these is a great political ruler, an enemy of Christ—he is against Christ. The other is a religious ruler who will imitate Christ and cause the world to worship the first beast, that is, to worship the political ruler. This is coming in the future, and everything this side of it is preparing the way for the coming of this one; so much so that when the political ruler and the religious ruler finally appear, the world will be ready for them. And it looks to me like the world is almost ready for them right now. To begin with, the political ruler will promise peace in the world, and for three and one-half years, he will do a pretty good job of it—but it is not permanent. It will build up to a mighty catastrophe that is ushered in by the war of Armageddon which will last for approximately three and one-half years until the coming of Christ to the earth to establish His kingdom.

At that time also, there will be one religion, and certainly we are moving in that direction even now. It will be a world religion where they will all pool their thinking. It will be a religion that doesn't really believe anything. There will be nothing to hold them together. We are so often urged today to get rid of that which separates us. My friend, if we get rid of all that separates us, there will not be anything left to hold us together. This is the problem with that type of thing. I am reminded of the story of the little boy who was walking down a jungle trail in Africa, carrying a polka dot umbrella. He met an elephant who said to him, "Where are you going, little boy?" The little boy said, "I'm not going anywhere," to which the elephant replied, "Well, I'm not either. Let me go with you." That is the kind of church union that is coming about today. They are going nowhere, they believe nothing, and therefore, they can all get together. This is the deceiver who is finally going to come, one to head up religion and one to head up the politics of this world. This is the Antichrist who is to come.

"For many deceivers are entered into the world." Gnosticism was running riot in John's day. Everywhere the Gospel has gone, the cults have always followed. The "isms" always follow the preaching of the Gospel—they never go before. There were coming along at that time quite a few of what was known as the Gnostic sect which was actually divided into many groups. There were the Cerinthian Gnostics who followed a teacher in Ephesus whose name was Cerinthus. There is a tradition that John, who was the pastor of the Ephesian church, went down to the public bath and saw old Cerinthus taking a bath also. So John got out of the pool, grabbed up his clothes, and didn't put them on until he got outside, because he wouldn't have anything to do with that heretic. Well, that is a tradition and may or may not be true, but it certainly expresses the viewpoint of John in his letter here. The Cerinthian Gnostics correspond to several of the cults today in that they taught that Jesus and Christ were two different entities altogether and that the divine came upon Jesus at His baptism and left Him at the cross. There were also the Docetic Gnostics who denied the reality of the physical body of Christ. They said that the apostles *thought* they saw Jesus, but He actually was not a real person; He was just an appearance. We have a few cults which have picked up that heresy also. This is the reason John said in his first epistle, "We have seen Him. We have heard Him. We've gazed upon Him. We've handled Him. We know what we are talking about, and He was a real man."

Then there were certain Jewish sects in that day, and when Christianity came along, they picked up a great deal of the Christian teachings. Evidently, there was a group of Essenes down at Qumran where they found the Dead Sea Scrolls. And at Masada, which fell in A.D. 73, three years after the fall of Jerusalem, there were about 967 zealots who had also picked up some of the teachings of Christ. Both groups had twisted, distorted, and warped conceptions of the person of Christ.

The thing that John is saying here and which is all-important today is that there are many deceivers who have entered into the world. They seem to have sort of centered right here in Southern California. This is a great incubation center for all kinds of false teachings. I used to say, as I spoke across this country, "I come from a land of flowers, fruits, and nuts—mostly religious nuts. I trust that you folk don't think that I am one of them!" The important thing is that the way you tell one who is true is by his viewpoint, his teaching, his beliefs concerning the person of the Lord Jesus Christ. Unless he thinks rightly of Him, everything else goes down the tube, and that person is a false teacher.

This does not mean that a person cannot hold a different view from what you and I would hold, for example, on election. Election has been a debatable point. John Wesley taught one thing, and John Calvin taught another viewpoint on it. But both of those men believed in the deity of Christ, and when you believe in the deity of Christ, it means you believe in the Virgin Birth, it means you believe the record that we have in the Word of God, and it means you believe in the apostles' doctrine which they taught in their epistles. There was a difference of opinion about election between these two men, but neither of them was a false teacher because both of them agreed on the essentials of the faith.

Let me use just one other illustration in this connection. I graduated and received my B.D. degree from my denominational seminary, as well as having done graduate work at Dallas Theological Seminary where I received my master's and doctor's degrees. That denominational school was amillennial, and they were dead set against the premillennial position. One of the professors and I became very good friends, and I admired him a great deal. That man could exalt the person of Christ. He could defend the virgin birth, the blood redemption, and the bodily resurrection of Christ in a way that I have heard no other person do. I actually sat in his classroom in tears as I heard him exalt the Lord Jesus. But he simply hated premillennialism. He didn't hate me—he and I were good friends. Because of the fact that he exalted Christ, I never felt we ought to separate or that I ought to break fellowship with him. He was no antichrist. He was a believer. He was an intellectual, and even they are wrong in some things, so I just took it for granted that he was wrong in that particular sphere. I am sure that someday, when he and I get to heaven, we will be in agreement. It may be that both of us will have to change a little relative to our beliefs concerning these secondary matters. I do consider them secondary when you put them down beside the person of Christ. It is what you think of Him that is all important.

John has emphasized that you are to walk according to the commandments of Christ, and the proof that you are a child of God is that you walk in love for the brethren. Now John has uttered a warning that many deceivers have come into the world. The believer today walks a very dangerous pathway through the world. To the left side of the pathway is the jungle of liberalism and apostasy. It is a beautiful but dangerous jungle because in it are beautiful but dangerous animals which are ready to devour us. I heard recently of a young man who had been in the armed forces and had had a real witness for Christ. But he apparently was lured to a seminary that destroyed his faith. This boy now has gone out into social service work, and his testimony is null and void. He is doing nothing but treading water. My heart goes out to a young fellow like that.

Then, on the opposite side of the pathway, there is a wilderness filled with rattlesnakes. It is the wilderness of extreme fundamentalism which is totally devoid of love. The only thing they think is important is to have the right doctrine. A brother may pat you on the back one day, but the next day, because you do not cross your t's or dot your i's as he does, he will attempt to destroy you by circulating a report in order to nullify your influence. Because of an overweening ambition, he will trample you underfoot. Your reputation is not safe in his hands, and he will exhibit hatred and bitterness rather than love toward you.

I have been in active Christian service since 1930, and I've met some of the great men of this century, giants of the faith who preached the truth. None of these men ever attempted to separate brethren or to dull the effectiveness of another's ministry by some slurring gossip. May I say to you, these men were great men, not only in doctrine but also in their lives. I have learned over the years that God's men who stand for the truth and who preach the Word of God, by and large, are men upon whom you can depend and who are very gracious in every manner.

I remember hearing this story of the late Dr. Harry Ironside when he was holding a conference at one of the prominent conference centers across this country. Some people go to these summer conferences for just one purpose, and that is to compare one speaker to another speaker and to try to set up some sort of conflict between them. I was told that a man came to Dr. Ironside at this conference and said to him, "Dr. Ironside, Dr. So-and-so was here last week and said such and such. But today you said the very opposite thing. Now which is correct?" The man was mentioning a minor point of doctrine. It was nothing vital but was simply a difference of opinion. All of us have differences of opinion, but we can differ without being disagreeable. So Dr. Ironside said to the man, "Well, I didn't know that Brother So-and-so taught that. That's quite interesting. Maybe I should look into it. I could be wrong." And then he walked away. The man stood there with his mouth open, because he surely couldn't get an argument there! May I say to you, I am confident that Dr. Ironside didn't feel that he was wrong, but he at least shut up that brother and kept him from trying to drive a wedge between brethren. This is the thing that, in my judgment, is actually more dangerous than liberalism. I can spot a liberal, and I can say truthfully that I do not associate or fellowship with them. I have nothing in common with them. At one time, I was accused falsely by extreme fundamentalists of fellowshiping with a certain bishop during an evangelistic campaign here in Southern California. The truth is that I never even met the man. I had no reason to. He and I were in two different spheres of activity altogether, and I had no fellowship with him. But I have found that the most dangerous ones for me are the extreme fundamentalists. I would say that I am more afraid of them. They prattle pious platitudes and claim that they have the truth. But woe unto the man who disagrees with them on minor matters, especially the matter of separation, as if that were the all-important issue. Their priorities are not doctrine but assassination of character and name-calling on the lowest level. I have met both ministers and members of churches who frighten me more than a rattlesnake. The venom of bitterness and jealousy and hatred was dripping from their mouths as they feigned their love and devotion to Christ and to the truth. The great message of 2 John is that truth walks in shoe leather, and if it does not, it is dangerous. My friend, we need to be very careful of both extremes of the spectrum of faith today.

John says that the way you are going to tell if one is not a child of God is: "Whosoever doeth not righteousness is not of God, neither he that loveth not his brother" (1 John 3:10). Love and righteousness are the two manifestations of a child of God. We are to be aware of those who are not believers, the deceivers who deny the deity of Christ. John is saying that if you deny the deity of Christ, you are not a Christian. You may be religious, but you are not a Christian—let's understand that. After all, *Christian* means one who is a follower of Christ, one who believes in Him. You cannot be a follower of Christ unless you believe in His virgin birth, unless you believe in His deity, His miraculous life, and His work of redemption upon the cross.

Look to yourselves, that we lose not those things which we have wrought, but that we receive a full reward [2 John 8].

You do not lose your salvation when you have fellowship with the wrong folk—we need to understand that very clearly—but you do put yourself in a dangerous position. It does mean that the minute you and I identify ourselves with a cult or go off into this type of thing which denies the deity of Christ, we have lost our reward. There will be no reward for a believer who has done this.

Every believer ought to be working for a reward, to be able to hear Him say someday, "Well done, thou good and faithful servant" (see Matt. 25:21). At the end of his life, Paul was able to say, "I have fought a good fight, I have finished my course, I have kept the faith: Henceforth there is laid up for me a crown of righteousness, which the Lord, the righteous judge, shall give me at that day . . ."(2 Tim. 4:7–8). During his life, he wasn't sure of it, for he said that he didn't want to be disapproved when he came into the presence of Christ. Therefore, it will behoove us to be very careful not to be taken in by deceivers.

Whosoever transgresseth, and abideth not in the doctrine of Christ, hath not God. He that abideth in the doctrine of Christ, he hath both the Father and the Son [2 John 9].

The word *transgresseth* is a very interesting word. In the Greek it is *proagō*. *Agō* means "to go"; *pro* means "before." *Proagō* means "to go before or to go ahead." Therefore, the meaning here is not so much to transgress as to go farther than is right. This is the meaning that Thayer gives in his Greek lexicon of the New Testament—to go farther than is right. "Whosoever goes farther than is right, that is, goes to some extreme." This is what the Gnostics claimed for themselves. The word *gnosis* means "knowledge." The Gnostics claimed to have a little more knowledge than anyone else, something that made them superduper saints. There are a few saints in that category today; they feel that they have something the rest of us don't have. Every now and then, I get a letter from some person who tells me I'm lacking somehow. I recognize that I am, but I don't feel they are the ones to tell me because they tell it from the viewpoint that *they* have it and I don't. They feel like they are superduper, and they manifest no love for the brethren, which means they are not abiding in the doctrine of Christ. This is the thing that characterizes them.

In my Southland there were a group of people when I was a boy who we: known as Holy Rollers. I attended several of their meetings when I was a young fellow just for the entertainment of watching them roll, and they actually rolled. Yet they preached the Gospel, and many of them were real believers. Bishop Moore of the old Southern Methodist church was at a conference of Methodist preachers where he was approached by a young country preacher who asked, "Bishop Moore, do you think the Holy Rollers will go to heaven?" The bishop replied, "They will if they don't run past the place!" It seems to me that that is the condition of which John is speaking here: Whosoever goes farther than is right, whoever becomes an extremist "and abideth not in the doctrine of Christ, hath not God."

I was reading sometime ago about several theologians in the East who met with a group of preachers. Together they came to the conclusion that they no longer needed to answer the fundamentalists on the question of the virgin birth of Christ or the deity of Christ or whether Christ died for our sins. They feel like they have graduated from that. They have become highly intellectual, totally sanctified, and have reached the summum bonum of life. They are now up at the apex, looking down on all the rest of us poor folk who believe in the deity of Christ and His death for our sins. To my judgment they have transgressed, abide not in the doctrine of Christ, and have not God. No wonder they came to the conclusion that God was dead! But He wasn't dead. They were dead—"dead in trespasses and sins" (see Eph. 2:1). "Whosoever transgresseth, and abideth not in the doctrine of Christ, hath not God."

"He that abideth in the doctrine of Christ, he hath both the Father and the Son." If you are abiding in the doctrine of Christ, you have God the Father, and you have God the Son, and you have access to the Father through the Son. We have access to God through Christ, by His marvelous, infinite grace if we abide in the doctrine of Christ.

The word abide means "to remain"—this is a permanent arrangement. Someone told me that he had asked a liberal preacher in Los Angeles years ago what he thought about me. This liberal preacher is an outstanding man, a very fine man in many ways. I have always respected him because he is one of the few honest liberals I have met. He just came out and said that he believed practically nothing, and he stuck by his guns. I simply feel he should not be in the ministry. He is sort of like a man selling Fuller brushes who doesn't have any brushes to sell. This liberal preacher said, "Well I respect McGee and his viewpoint. The thing is that it's old-fashioned, and he hasn't changed it in years. He apparently hasn't grown a bit." May I say to you, that is about the nicest compliment the man could have returned to me because I haven't changed and I intend for it to be that way. John is saying here that he who abides in the doctrine of Christ, who remains in it and doesn't change, has both the Father and the Son.

If there come any unto you, and bring not this doctrine, receive him not into your house, neither bid him God speed [2 John 10].

I cannot think of a stronger statement than this. We need to recall the background of this letter again. John is writing to "the elect lady," who may have been an outstanding woman in the church, noted for her hospitality. Apparently, she is a woman of means who can entertain guests lavishly. She is very generous. Evidently, some of these Gnostics came by, and she entertained them. Then she was under conviction about it, and she wrote to John. What should she do in a case like that? Should she entertain them? She would feel badly if she turned them away. What really should be her attitude toward an apostate, toward a heretic, toward one who denies the deity of Christ but pretends to be a follower of Christ? Should she entertain him in her home?

We need to understand also that there were no Howard Johnson motels or Holiday Inns or Hilton Hotels or Ramada Inns in the Roman Empire. The little inns that they had were pretty bare places to stay. An inn was not even a place where you got a bed. You had to bring your own bed with you. All you did was rent a space to put down your little mat or pad on which you would sleep. Maybe there were people sleeping on both sides of you, at your head, and down at your feet—all around you. That was the method for travelers in that day. So the homes of believers were always open to traveling evangelists and Bible teachers in the days of the early church. When these men would arrive in a town, there would always be some home where they would be entertained. Remember how Paul stayed in the home of Aquila and Priscilla when he was in Corinth? That was the method in the early church and the general practice of the day.

I can remember when I was a boy in our little town in west Texas that my mother would invite a visiting preacher to come for dinner and sometimes to spend the night. My dad never liked that, I can tell you. He was not a believer, and he didn't care to have a preacher for dinner or to have him spend the night. We were poor folk, and so the preacher didn't get lavish entertainment. But he would usually get fried chicken, and my mother really knew how to fry chicken. That was the practice in our little town. Even up to this day, the Holiday Inn hasn't gotten there; in fact, there isn't a motel of any kind or description there. In that day the preacher was entertained in the home, but today my recommendation to you is to entertain him in a motel or hotel. That would be the proper way to do it today. The average minister needs a great deal of privacy for study and prayer, and he cannot get it when he is entertained in a home. However, I must say that there are a few homes across this country that I have always enjoyed going into, because I can make myself at home and I feel at home there. They just let me do what I need and want to do, and it is a joy to be there.

This woman to whom John is writing is a woman of hospitality, and she has this question about entertaining false teachers. John lays it on the line here: "If there come any unto you, and bring not this doctrine, receive him not into your house, neither bid him God speed."

Now John says something else that ought to alert everyone of us today—

For he that biddeth him God speed is partaker of his evil deeds [2 John 11].

If you entertain a false teacher, if you support him, you are a partner with him in his deeds. This is the reason that you ought to investigate everything that you give to as a Christian, because if you are giving to the wrong thing, God considers you a partner in it.

The Lord Jesus gave a parable in this connection in which He told about a man who was working for another man and was about to be fired (see Luke 16:1–13). The man called in all his employer's creditors and offered them a discount if they would pay their bills, which they, of course, were glad to accept. He did this so that after he was fired he would be able to appeal to them for help since he had helped them. That was crooked—our Lord did not say it was right; He made it clear that it was wrong. He said, "The children of this world are in their generation wiser than the children of light." They are clever out yonder in the business world. There's many a man trying to make a fast buck today. It is a case of dog-eat-dog. Therefore, if the man in the world is wise about the way he invests his money and the way he uses his money, what about you, Christian friend? Are you moved by some sentimental story, and do you give because of that? Are you moved by a picture of a few orphans, of little children in foreign countries? Do you know that your money is getting to them? Are you motivated today by sentiment? If you are a partner in that which denies the deity of the Lord Jesus Christ and all that He is and stands for and all that He did for us, if you are supporting that sort of thing, God will hold you responsible for it. He said that the children of the world are wiser than we are. We ought to get smart. We ought to wise up to this and not be taken in by it. Charity has become a big racket today. Collecting money under false pretenses is one of the biggest rackets there is. This is the reason I sometimes mention that I haven't yet started an orphans' home for stray cats in the Aleutian Islands! In fact, I don't know whether there are any cats up there or not. My business is giving out the Word of God, and I hope this is your business, too.

PERSONAL GREETING

Having many things to write onto you, I would not write with paper and ink: but I trust to come unto you, and speak face to face, that our joy may be full.

The children of thy elect sister greet thee. Amen [2 John 12–13].

In other words, John says, "I can tell it better than I can write it." David said the same thing, ". . . my tongue is the pen of a ready writer" (Ps. 45:1). When David began to write that wonderful forty-fifth psalm, a psalm of praise to Christ, he simply said, "I wish I could *tell* it to you. I can *say* it better than I can write it." This is the reason I love the radio ministry. I can say it lots better than I can write it.

"The children of thy elect sister greet thee. Amen." Apparently, they were children of a sister of this elect lady, or it was a sister church sending greetings to this lady and to the local church there.

This is a tremendous little letter, and its message ought to alert every believer today.

(For Bibliography to 2 John, see Bibliography at the end of 3 John, page 61.)

3 JOHN

The Third Epistle of
JOHN

INTRODUCTION

The writer of this little epistle is John the apostle. I rather face-tiously call this epistle "three-eyed John" because a very fine black preacher whom I knew years ago in the South called John's epistles "one-eyed John," "two-eyed John," and "three-eyed John." I don't know of a better way of remembering these epistles than this. This epistle, therefore, is "three-eyed John."

It is now the belief of some expositors that John wrote these epistles last—after he wrote the Book of Revelation. I'm rather inclined to agree with that viewpoint. This means that these epistles were written close to the end of the first century, somewhere between A.D. 90–100, but it would be very difficult to date them exactly. John probably wrote all three epistles very close together. I don't think there would be much difference in time from one epistle to the other.

In his first epistle, John emphasizes the fact that the family of God is held together by love and that the little children are to love one an-other. He makes it very clear that if they don't love one another, they are not God's children. Children have a love for those who are in their family—that is the normal thing even in natural relationships down here on this earth.

In the second epistle, however, John puts up a tremendous warning that there are apostates, there are many antichrists, and there are many deceivers in the world. He says that a child of God is not to love them. We are not to be concerned with their welfare in the sense of entertain-ing them in our homes. The child of God is to keep a very close account and to make sure that those he entertains, those he supports, are true to the Word of God; that is, that they believe in the deity of Christ, that they believe that He is God manifest in the flesh. John wrote, "And the Word was made flesh . . ." (John 1:14). He had already said that the Word was God. Therefore, Jesus Christ is God manifest in the flesh. He is God dwelling, tabernacling in human flesh. Until a person believes that, he doesn't have a Savior. If Jesus Christ is just a man and that is all that He is, we do not have a Savior. There is no reason to remember His birth and no reason to remember His death or resurrection if He is just a man. It is all-important to recognize that He is God manifest in the flesh and that His work on the cross was a work that has power to save us. There is power in the blood because of who He is and because He died and rose again bodily. Those who deny these truths are not to be extended the fellowship or the support of the church. John goes so far in the second epistle as to say that believers are not to even bid such a person Godspeed. John said not to help him on his way or give him support. If you do, you are a partaker of his evil deeds, and you are a partner with him. Therefore, it behooves a child of God to know whom he supports.

As we come now to the third epistle, there is a similarity to John's second letter in some ways. It is very personal in character, and it carries the same theme of truth. Truth again is presented as all-important. When truth and love come into conflict, truth must survive. This means that you are not to love the false teacher. Walking in truth is all-important.

However, this third letter differs from the second in other ways. As you will note from the Outline which follows, this epistle deals with personalities. Also, in the second epistle, John says that the truth is worth standing for, but in this third epistle, John's emphasis is that the truth is worth working for. Someone has put it like this: "My life in God—that's salvation. My life with God—that's communion and fellowship. But my life for God—that's service." This epistle deals with my life for God, and it has to do with walking and working in the truth. Love can become very sloppy; it can become misdirected, and it certainly can be misunderstood if it is not expressed within the boundary of truth.

OUTLINE

I. **Gaius, Beloved Brother in the Early Church, Verses 1–8**
   (Gaius, the one to whom the letter is addressed, is urged to extend hospitality to true teachers of the Word.)

II. **Diotrephes, "who loveth to have the preeminence," Verses 9–11**
   (Evil deeds are an expression of false doctrine.)

III. **Demetrius "hath good report of all men, and of the truth itself," Verses 12–14**
   (A good life is an expression of true doctrine.)

3 JOHN

Years ago I preached a sermon on the subject, "You Will Find Them in the Yellow Pages," in which I dealt with two men from this little epistle of 3 John—Diotrephes and Demetrius—and with Demas whom Paul spoke of in 2 Timothy 4:10 (see also Col. 4:14; Philem. 23–24). Demas had been a fellow laborer with Paul but had deserted the work; he loved the world and departed from Paul. My sermon was about Demas, Diotrephes, and Demetrius—each of their names begins with a D. I probably should have included Gaius who is also mentioned in this epistle—and if his name had been Daius, I'm sure I would have! Modern advertising tells us that we can always find it in the Yellow Pages. It does not matter whether you want to purchase an aardvark or a zebra, an atom splitter or a zymometer, an abacus or a zygote, you will find it in the Yellow Pages. If we could get ahold of the Yellow Pages of the Roman Empire in the first century, we would probably find these men listed there. However, we do find them in the Word of God, and they give us the answer to some very interesting questions. How did the believers of the first century make out? How were they holding out at the close of the first century? Did they all become martyrs? Were they all paragons of virtue? Were they all worthy followers of Christ? Were they worthy examples of the faith? Among the millions who turned to Christ in the first three centuries, how did the average believer turn out? Well, here in this epistle we find two who were outstanding men of God—Gaius and Demetrius. These men really stood for the faith of God. We also find one who was not outstanding. Diotrephes was not standing at all; he was doing anything but standing for the truth.

GAIUS—A DELIGHTFUL BROTHER

The elder unto the well-beloved Gaius, whom I love in the truth [3 John 1].

"The elder." As he did in the second epistle, John adopts the term *elder*. It could refer to his age. He is in his nineties, and certainly he is a presbyter, an elder, in the sense of age. He is a senior citizen at this time. Also, *elder* speaks of an officer in the early church, and certainly John could claim that. In fact, he could have claimed more. He could have said, "I am an apostle," but he doesn't do that. Gaius is a friend, and you don't write that way to your friend. At least, I don't write that way to very personal friends. I write to several fellows with whom I was in school and who are old men now—I'm the only one who has managed to stay young, but they've gotten old! I call each one of them by his first name, and when I sign my name, I don't mention the title *Doctor* at all—those fellows would laugh at me. I simply write my name, Vernon or Mac. I was called Mac when I was in college and seminary. I go by that appellation, and so I just sign that way. John is writing to a personal friend, and he simply says, "The elder unto the well-beloved Gaius."

"Unto the well-beloved Gaius"—I love that. John's letter is addressed to a believer in the early church by the name of Gaius. Gaius was a beloved brother in the church. Four times John calls him "beloved" (vv. 1, 2, 5, 11). John knows and loves him in the Lord, and he now writes a letter to this brother who apparently is in some local church.

"Whom I love in the truth," Immediately we are told that Gaius is sound in doctrine. He accepted the deity of Christ. Gaius is a man who stood for the truth, and he not only stood for the truth but he also worked for the truth. Here is a man who walked and worked in love. He manifested love. You have to think right if you are going to act right—that is true in any sphere of life today.

Beloved, I wish above all things that thou mayest prosper and be in health, even as thy soul prospereth [3 John 2].

"Beloved"—John evidently thought a great deal of Gaius and was very close to him since, again, he calls him "beloved."

"I wish above all things that thou mayest prosper and be in health."

Very frankly, John makes it clear that he wants Gaius to prosper not only financially (he apparently was a man of means), but John also says, "I want you to prosper in your health." Evidently, Gaius was not a well man.

"Even as thy soul prospereth." And John wanted him to prosper also in his soul, to grow spiritually. There are a lot of Christians today who are sick spiritually. They have good health physically, but they have pretty bad health spiritually. It is certainly well for a child of God to have both. Good health physically is wonderful to have—many of us didn't appreciate it until we lost it. And it is important to have good health spiritually. What physical health is to the body, holiness is to the spiritual life of the believer. To be healthy spiritually is holiness; it is to be growing in grace and in the knowledge of Christ.

There were traveling around in that day many men who were teaching the Word of God and doing missionary work. Gaius would open his home to them and entertain them. He was not only a large-hearted man, he not only walked in love, but he also walked in truth, and he tested these teachers. And in spite of his poor health, he was able to be very active in hospitality.

For I rejoiced greatly, when the brethren came and testi-fied of the truth that is in thee, even as thou walkest in the truth [3 John 3].

Many of these traveling evangelists and missionaries reported to John the graciousness of Gaius and his walk in the truth. They said, "When you go to the church where Gaius is one of the leaders, you will find he is a very wonderful man. He is not only a man of means but also a very generous man. I was entertained in his home." In that day they didn't put the traveling preacher in a Howard Johnson's or a Ramada Inn because there weren't any. If there had been, I believe they would have put him there. But generally, the little inns in the Roman Empire were flea-bitten places, dirty, and sometimes very sinful; so the custom of that day was to entertain these men in homes.

"For I rejoiced greatly, when the brethren came and testified of the truth that is in thee, even as thou walkest in the truth." This is the testimony that other brethren gave concerning Gaius. This was their judgment of him. "The truth" is actually the doctrine and the teaching of the apostles. The article should be omitted: "walkest in truth." This refers not only to doctrine but also to his conduct. The mark of the believer is to walk in truth. Truth is that which is dominant. The *summum bonum* for the Christian is whether or not he is walking in the truth and walking in the light. It isn't how you walk but where you walk that is important. Are you walking in the truth? Walking in the truth also means walking in the right conduct or walking in love of the brethren.

Those who were out in a teaching ministry in the early church would come to Gaius' town and to his church, and they would find that his home was wide open to true brethren. Gaius had a spiritual discernment. He could tell who were the genuine believers and who were not. After all, all you need to do is to make sure about a man's relationship to the person of Jesus Christ.

> What think ye of Christ? is the test
> To try both your state and your scheme.
> You cannot be right in the rest
> Unless you think rightly of Him.
> —Author unknown

You must think rightly of Him in order to be right in everything else. These brethren testified, "Brother Gaius tested us out. He found out whether we believed in the deity of Christ. He found out whether we believed in the Virgin Birth and whether we believed that Christ died a redemptive death upon the cross and was raised bodily from the grave. When he found out that we did believe these things, he opened his home and received us and discovered that we also had a love for the brethren. And then his heart was open to us." What a marvelous testimony Gaius had!

I have no greater joy than to hear that my children walk in truth [3 John 4].

This is a great comfort. This is wonderful encouragement. "I have no greater joy than to hear that my children walk in truth." John had been the pastor of the church in Ephesus and had led many to the Lord. It is a great joy to him, now that he is an old man, to hear that his converts, scattered out over the area of Asia, are still walking in truth. Here again "walking in truth" means walking in right doctrine and in love for the brethren—his children manifested these things.

It is a great joy to me today to get letters from those who were led to the Lord over the years of my ministry. They say, "We are still walking in the truth," and perhaps they tell about how they are in a Bible church and are attempting to serve the Lord. That brings joy to my heart. When I hear of young ministers who used to be in my classes and who are now standing for the truth, that brings joy to the heart. My daughter is like a great many other young people today. She thinks her dad is just a little old fogy, more or less a back number. The other day she went out to hear a young man whom I had the privilege of teaching. After she and her husband had gone to hear him, she came back to tell me how wonderful he was and what a glorious message he brought. She told me what the message was as if it was something I had never heard before. It did sound strangely familiar, but I never said anything to my daughter—I just listened as she told me how wonderful it was. Then she said, "You know, Dad, you may not be able to speak to young people today, but he is able to speak to young people, and they listen to him. His church is filled with young people." Well, I couldn't help but smile. I didn't really want to tell her that that fellow's message just happened to be one of my messages. I was glad that he gave it. I am sure that my daughter has heard me give it, but it didn't mean anything when Dad gave it because I'm an old fogy. But this young, sharp boy put in a lot of new words that young people use today that aren't a part of my vocabulary, and of all things, it is just a brand-new message! Do you think I feel badly over that? You do not know what great joy that brought to me in my heart. I know exactly how John felt. John says, "I have no greater joy than to hear that my children walk in truth." Isn't that wonderful? You cannot help but rejoice in that, especially when you have come to the sundown period of life and you know that your future is no longer ahead of you. My future is behind me, and

I rejoice in these young preachers who are coming along. And to feel that maybe I had a little part in their training and to know that young people are crowding in to hear them is a wonderful thing.

Beloved, thou doest faithfully whatsoever thou doest to the brethren, and to strangers [3 John 5].

Gaius was evidently one of the children of John, one of John's converts. His conduct conforms to his doctrine, and it is marvelous when that takes place.

From verse 5 to 8, John commends Gaius for having received and entertained the true teachers of the Word. Let me draw the contrast: In 2 John the apostle warns against receiving false teachers, but in 3 John he encourages the believers to receive the true brethren. Just because you have been deceived and stung for awhile ought not to keep you from receiving the true brethren. I know a lady who supports our radio ministry in a very wonderful way. She is down on the church, and I recently found out why. She happens to be a widow and a very attractive person. She went to a couple of churches where the pastors made a pass at her. Believe me, that turned her off, and she now has nothing to do with the church. Frankly, I have urged her to get into a good Bible church where there are real men of God who will not be doing that sort of thing. Many of us have been disappointed and deceived by false brethren, but we should not let that deter us from supporting that which we believe is of the Lord. This woman gives support only to radio ministries today. Very frankly, I think she's wrong. I don't think she is wrong to support radio—don't misunderstand me—but I do feel that one or two sour experiences ought not to sour you against the church.

John tells us in his second epistle that many deceivers have gone out into the world. Why not be like Gaius and have a little discernment? Don't support anything—including a church or a radio ministry—until you are sure that it is of God. Be sure that the Word of God is being given out. Be sure that they love the brethren (and that they don't love the "sistern" too much!). John is talking about things that are very practical today. He is really getting down to the nitty-gritty, right down where the rubber meets the road, right down where the ball hits the bat. He is encouraging Gaius to support the true brethren in the Lord.

> **Which have borne witness of thy charity before the church: whom if thou bring forward on their journey after a godly sort, thou shalt do well [3 John 6].**

These brethren would return from a trip to John's church. I have a notion that when they came together for the purpose of worship, John would say, "Well, I see Brother So-and-so. He's been out evangelizing, and we'd like to have a word from him. We'd like to have a report as to how the Lord led him and how the Lord blessed him." Brother So-and-so would get up and give his report, and he would say, "When I came to this place there was a brother there by the name of Gaius, and he is a choice servant of God. He opened his home to me, but he doesn't do that for everybody because he certainly examined me. He made an inspection of me to make sure I was teaching the Word of God. He wanted to know whether or not I believed the Word of God and whether or not I was walking in love. He tested me and found that I was, and then he just opened up his heart and home to me, and we had wonderful fellowship." Now John is writing to Gaius, and he says, "I have heard this now from several, and I want you to know how much it delights my heart."

"Whom if thou bring forward on their journey after a godly sort, thou shalt do well." In the second epistle, John says that if you bid Godspeed to false teachers, you are a partaker with them, you are guilty of their deeds. But now he says that if you help those who are giving out the Word of God and who are walking in love, you do well. This is actually something you *should* be doing. Why?—

> **Because that for his name's sake they went forth, taking nothing of the Gentiles [3 John 7].**

John writes to Gaius, "These brethren went forth, trusting the Lord, and you opened up your home to them. They are genuine, they are real, and you received them." These men went out at great sacrifice. They didn't receive a salary; they didn't receive any remuneration. They went out trusting the Lord, and homes were opened to them. In some places they were given support; in other places they were not.

"Taking nothing of the Gentiles." This my friend, is another way of testing that which is genuine or not. Are you supporting something that is simply a religious racket for money, something that is trying to get every Tom, Dick, and Harry to donate to the cause? Or is it a work of the Lord that depends on the Lord's people? John says that these true men would take nothing of the Gentiles, that is, from unbelievers.

I always try to make it clear on our radio broadcast that we are just asking believers to support the program. If an unbeliever is listening, we'd rather he not give. We hope he listens; we hope he sends for the literature, but very frankly, I do not really believe God can bless what an unbeliever gives. We believe the scriptural method is to ask only believers to give. These men went forth, taking nothing from the Gentiles. They would not appeal to unbelievers to give to the Lord's work. I know there are many who disagree, but I do not believe that unbelievers should be asked to support the Lord's work. As the ark went through the wilderness, it was carried on the shoulders of the Israelite priests. They could not even put it on a cart. God said that the priests were to carry it. And God's priests today are His believers. Every believer is a priest, and you and I are to carry the Lord Jesus Christ into this world today. Therefore, we do not ask unbelievers to give, but we do ask believers to give—especially those who not only believe in Christ but who also believe that we are giving out the Word of God today. And we do not apologize for asking believers to give because we believe that the Lord's work is to be carried forward in this method.

We therefore ought to receive such, that we might be fellow-helpers to the truth [3 John 8].

In other words, you would be a partner with these men if you opened your home to them, if you supported them and helped them on their way. In the second epistle, John warns "the elect lady" not to receive apostates into her home because if she does, she is a partner with them in their evil deeds. Now that warning might cause someone just to shut his home and not receive true brethren either; that is, some might shut up their homes to all who might come in order to make sure that they did not entertain false teachers. But John says, "Wait just a minute. If they are men walking in the light, if they are men walking in love, and if they are men who have the life of God within them, you should receive them." I think you can tell when a man is speaking by the Holy Spirit. I am sure there was better discernment in the early church than there is in the church today. I am confident that, although we may know more Bible than they did, we certainly do not have the spiritual discernment that they did. But when a man is doing God's work, he should be supported. "That we might be fellow-helpers to the truth." When Gaius helped them along, he became a partner with them in getting out the Word of God.

DIOTREPHES—A DICTATOR

Gaius was such a wonderful fellow, one of those choice saints in the early church. You could wish that all of the men in the early church were like that, but I am sorry to have to report that they were not. We come now to another man, Diotrephes, and this is what John has to say of him—

I wrote unto the church: but Diotrephes, who loveth to have the preeminence among them, receiveth us not [3 John 9].

John wrote a pentateuch of the New Testament (just as Moses wrote the Pentateuch of the Old Testament); John wrote a gospel, the Revelation, and three epistles. That makes five books—he wrote a pentateuch. If it is true that John wrote his epistles after the Book of the Revelation, this epistle is his swan song. It was written toward the close of the first century, and by that time, many wonderful believers had been brought into the truth and into the church. We might wonder how they got along. Were they all paragons of virtue? Were they all outstanding men of God? Were they worthy followers of Christ? Well, there were some like Gaius, real men of God, men of courage, outstanding men who stood for the things of God. However, there were also men like this man Diotrephes. He is a very different type of individual from Gaius. The thing that marks Diotrephes is that he loved to have the preeminence. Gaius is the delightful brother, but Diotrephes is the dictator. It is said that he even opposed the apostle John. John had written to this church to receive certain men, among whom was an outstanding preacher of the Gospel, one of those unknown saints of God, whose name was Demetrius, but this man Diotrephes would not receive him. As I have mentioned previously, the early Christians practiced hospitality. Peter mentions it in 1 Peter 4:9, "Use hospitality one to another without grudging." Paul also talks about it in 1 Timothy 5:9–10; Romans 12:13; and Titus 1:8. I do not know whether Diotrephes was a preacher or a layman in his church, but he would not even open his home to any of these men whom John had recommended. The reason is that he loved to have the preeminence. His motto was "to rule or ruin." He was going to have his own way, and it did not make any difference what the result might be.

In verse 8 John urged, "We therefore ought to receive such, that we might be fellow-helpers to the truth." May I say to you, there is a real compulsion today upon the child of God to support those who are giving out the Word of God. If you have a preacher who is doing that, you should support him. That was the practice in the early church.

Diotrephes is a man who puts on airs. He is pretentious. He is vainglorious. He struts around as a peacock. He has an overweening ambition. He is puffed up, inflated like a balloon. He is one whom you have to receive with a flourish of trumpets. He comes in in a blaze of glory. That's Diotrephes. John will bring five charges against him: (1) He must occupy the leading place in the church; (2) he actually refused to receive John; (3) he made malicious statements against the apostles; (4) he refused to entertain the missionaries, the ones who were traveling through the country (and the reason obviously is that he wanted to do the speaking and teaching himself); and (5) he excommunicated those who did entertain the missionaries. In other words, Diotrephes wanted to be the first exalted ruler of the church. Woe unto you if you attempted to oppose him. If he was a layman, I sure feel sorry for his pastor. I am of the opinion he tried to keep his pastor under his thumb in order that he could preside. He wanted to be the one to be heard. Diotrephes was a man who was self-opinionated. He was self-exalting instead of self-effacing. I am sure that he would have claimed to have been a self-made man instead of having let the Holy Spirit make him over. He was self-sufficient, and I think he was guilty of self-admiration also. He was self-willed, self-satisfied, and self-confident. He felt that he could do all the teaching and preaching and that he did not need these other men to come and minister.

As I am saying all of this, I wonder if you recognize this fellow. In many churches today, there are men like Diotrephes, men who want to run the church. I am no longer a pastor of a church, and I can say frankly what I think and what I know to be true. I'm not speaking of any theory whatsoever but of what I know from experience over the years. I have met men who, although they put up a very pious front, have tried to run the church. I have known men like that in churches I have served but, thank the Lord, I never had much trouble with them. Sometimes it is a little clique which will do anything in order to rule. I have watched such people wreck church after church—a little group or an individual like Diotrephes who loves to have the preeminence.

I am going to say something now that may be very harsh. There are many men who may mean well but who enjoy leading in the church. They enjoy being up before a group of people. For the most part, the ones I have met are almost Bible ignoramuses—they know very little about the Word of God. But they love to talk, and their talk has actually sometimes caused me to bow my head in shame as I was sitting there on the platform. Some of the things they say are totally unscriptural, totally beside the point, and dead as a doornail. Then they wonder why their church is losing members. They wonder why people are not coming. It is very evident why. There are many who ought to keep quiet in the church. Remember that Paul said, "Study to be quiet" (see 1 Thess. 4:11). Instead of trying to teach young people to talk, we ought to teach them to keep quiet because we have many older ones today who talk too much. My friend, we ought not to talk in church unless we have something to say, unless we have something *from* God to say.

Many folk want to be up front in church. Not only have I met Dio-trephes, but I have also met Mrs. Diotrephes in the church today. May I say that there are certain people who ought not to sing solos in the church. They do not bring glory to God, and sometimes they select songs which absolutely hurt the service rather than help it. My friend, you ought to search your heart before God before you stand up in the church and begin to sing or talk. Some soloists like to make a little talk before they sing a song. Many times the message they bring is just about as phony as anything can be. They want to tell you why they are going to sing that particular song. Why not just sing the song? If the song has a message, that is all the message a soloist needs to give.

I say all this because I am deeply concerned. I once had the oppor-tunity to observe the moviemakers out here in Hollywood as they worked on the filming of a scene. When I got tired of watching and left, they had already shot that one scene *fifteen* times, and they were still working on it! I thought as I left, *Oh, if only God's people would work as hard to do everything in the church service to bring glory to the name of Christ!* It all deserves the best we've got, my friend.

All of us need to search our hearts—even the ministers. Why are you presiding? Why are you leading? Why do you sing? Do you love to have the preeminence? Are you doing this for the glory of God? Cer-tainly we need somebody to preside. We need somebody to sing a solo. We need somebody to teach the Word. Many are needed, but search your heart before you do anything because you can wreck a church if you are one like Diotrephes who loves to have the preeminence.

Mrs. McGee and I were ministering in a certain church where they did not have a pastor at the time. When we left after the service, she said to me concerning the man who presided, "He certainly did enjoy presiding, didn't he?" I replied, "Yes, he loved it, and I'm wondering whether they *really* are seeking for a pastor with that man presiding." He was not only presiding, he was killing the church. The attendance was way down. I felt very sorry for the pastor who would come to the church because he certainly was going to have trouble with that indi-vidual.

John now says that he is going to deal with this problem—

> Wherefore, if I come, I will remember his deeds which
> he doeth, prating against us with malicious words: and
> not content therewith, neither doth he himself receive
> the brethren, and forbiddeth them that would, and cas-
> teth them out of the church [3 John 10].

"Wherefore, if I come"—I do not think this is the *if* of doubt. We shall
see at the end of the epistle that John intends to come and he is coming.
But we never know what a day will bring forth. John says, "If I come,"
in the sense of, "If something should come up, if something should
happen, I might be unable to make the trip." But his intentions are to
come. There is no doubt in his mind about that.

"I will remember his deeds which he doeth." In Christianity, the
important word is *truth*, and truth manifests itself in love—it is just as
simple as that and as important as that. Diotrephes loved to have the
preeminence which, by the way, is a characteristic of the flesh. The
fruit of the Spirit is meekness, but Diotrephes was a dictator. Meekness
does not necessarily mean weakness or cowardice. Someone has said,
"Silence is golden, but sometimes it is yellow." It is too bad there
weren't those in the church who spoke out against Diotrephes. Moses
was considered a meek man, but when he got up and talked to the
children of Israel, he didn't sound like a meek man according to our
notion of meekness. He spoke with the authority God had given him.
The Lord Jesus was meek and lowly, but He went in and cleansed the
temple. This is the reason I feel I should speak out on this because
nobody else speaks along these lines as far as I know. When this thing
is hurting our churches, somebody should say, "Look brother, sit
down. You are spoiling things. You ought not to be loving the preeminence all the time. You should learn to be meek and let others speak."
John says, "Wherefore, if I come, I will remember his deeds which he
doeth." Diotrephes exhibits that which is not the mark of a believer, by
any means. He apparently did not have the truth.

"Prating against us with malicious words." Diotrephes was attempting to completely destroy the effectiveness of the apostles and
especially of John. John says, "When I get there, I'm going to deal with

him. I'm going to speak out against him. I'm going to let it be known that this man is using malicious words."

A man called me sometime ago who was a member of a church that I served at one time. He wept as he said, "I want you to forgive me for saying the things I said about you." He had gone so far as to say that I had left the church in debt. I have never left in debt any church that I have served. The fact of the matter is that I left that church with a tremendous reserve fund, but he, along with a few others, simply did not mention that. As a result, a false report went out. I told him, "You don't have to ask me to forgive you. You need to ask the Lord's forgiveness." He said, "I've already repented and talked to Him." I told him, "It would be nice if you would now give the true report to those you gave the false report." He had been a Diotrephes. He enjoyed presiding. He enjoyed having his way. Apparently, a change has come over him now. He is in another church, and I understand that he is doing a good job. I rejoice in that. But he was a Diotrephes. I feel that I should have dealt with him more severely than I did when I was there because John says, "I intend to deal with Diotrephes."

"And not content therewith, neither doth he himself receive the brethren, and forbiddeth them that would, and casteth them out of the church." Imagine this fellow! He is excommunicating anybody who would entertain these men John had recommended. What a horrible picture this is! If you want to wreck a church, just have a man like this or a little group like this and, my friend, you will wreck the church. The sad situation is that there are too many men like this today in Christian circles.

You can call John an apostle of love if you want to, but the Lord Jesus called him a son of thunder. I think they had a regular thunderstorm when John arrived at this church because he said he was going to deal with Diotrephes. It is too bad other churches don't deal with Diotrephes, because he will wreck a church if he is permitted to go on.

Beloved, follow not that which is evil, but that which is good. He that doeth good is of God: but he that doeth evil hath not seen God [3 John 11].

John encourages Gaius to continue doing that which is good. Again, he emphasizes that the one who practices righteousness is a child of God but the one who does not practice righteousness is not born of God.

DEMETRIUS—A DEPENDABLE BROTHER

We come now to the third man, Demetrius. He is a lovely fellow. You just cannot help but rejoice in him. Gaius is a delightful brother, Diotrephes is a dictator, and now we will find Demetrius to be a dependable brother.

> **Demetrius hath good report of all men, and of the truth itself: yea, and we also bear record; and ye know that our record is true [3 John 12].**

"Demetrius hath good report of all men and of the truth itself." Here is a man sound in the faith. "Yea, and we also bear record." In the mouth of two witnesses, a thing is established. Demetrius has a good report of all men; the truth bears witness to him, and John says, "I bear witness also." "And ye know that our record is true." This church knows that John bears a true witness.

Demetrius is obviously one of these wonderful saints of God whom Diotrephes had shut out of the church. We have only one verse about Demetrius—this is all we know. He is never mentioned again in Scripture. However, this one verse of Scripture gives us an insight into the Christian character of this noble saint of God. We cannot identify him with any other of the same name. His name means "belonging to Demeter," that is, Ceres, the goddess of agriculture. This identifies him as a convert from paganism. He evidently was brought up in a pagan home and worshipped the gods of the Greeks and Romans. This man, converted, now goes around teaching the Word of God. He adorned the doctrine of Christ. Others testified to his character, and he was true to the doctrine of Scripture.

Demetrius is evidently among the group of men whom John mentions that Diotrephes was not receiving. He is one of the itinerant preachers who went about in the first century—humble, unknown, and unsung. He is a member of that great army which carried the Gospel throughout the Roman Empire so that it could be said that the whole world had heard the Gospel. The whole Roman world of that day, the whole civilized world, was entirely evangelized. They were pushing out beyond its borders when the apostasy began to set in, when there came in men like Diotrephes.

Demetrius is one of the shining lights of the New Testament, a humble saint of God. Around us today, there are multitudes of people like him. They are not a Diotrephes. And they are not even a Gaius—they are not outstanding Christians. They are just humble saints of God, doing the thing God has called them to do. In a humble way, they are maybe just teaching a little Sunday school class. I heard the other day about one who teaches the handicapped. How wonderful that is, but nobody knows about her. Nobody has ever given her a loving cup. They ought to, but they never have. She doesn't want it, and she would be embarrassed if you gave her one. There are many saints of God like that today. God is using them in a small way. They are not trying to be the chief soloist; they are just singing in the choir. They don't try to be the main speaker. They don't want to preside. They don't want to be the chairman of every board in the church. They are willing just to fade into the woodwork of the church. But they are pillars of the church. They are supporting the work, and they are encouraging the preacher.

One of the most wonderful church members I ever knew was a dear little lady who came in every Sunday morning on a cane. She never missed a Sunday morning, and she always had something nice to say. She was always encouraging the preacher. She told me one time, "I think that's my job. It's all I can do." Well, she did other things, too. The church is filled with wonderful saints of God. Don't get the impression that I think that everybody in the church is a Diotrephes. Thank God that there are very few of them. In this epistle here, it is two good men to one bad. I think the average is better than that today in the church—I think maybe it is one hundred to one. Thank God for the Demetrius folk in our churches today.

The tense that John uses here indicates that Demetrius had a good reputation in the past and that he still has a good reputation. Over a long period, Demetrius has demonstrated a time-tested faith. He is Demetrius, the dependable brother. The church knows him as a man of God. Now you might deceive the church, but Demetrius was tested by the truth. He measures up to the definition of a believer. John knows him and agrees. There are three witnesses to the fact that Demetrius adorns the doctrine of Christ.

The real test of the Christian life is not in the arena backed by applause. It was not before the crowd in the Colosseum. There were five million martyrs who bore testimony to the truth of the Gospel in the first three centuries and who laid down their lives for Christ. Did you know that there were many more millions who bore witness by the faithful lives they lived each day? Nothing spectacular, nothing sensational, nothing outstanding—they just lived for God. They had a purpose, they had a direction, and they had a thrilling experience. (Our contemporary civilization is experiencing a decadence that characterized Rome in the first century. After World War II, an Englishman wrote the play, *Look Back in Anger*. It revealed a bottomless pessimism without any hope for the future. This attitude produced the Beatle-brained mob of youth we have today who are without direction. Three young people I met in Athens told me they simply wanted to drop out of society.) Into the decadent first century, with its low morals and erosion of character, there came the message from God that He had given His Son. There were multitudes who came into contact with Him, and they got involved. May I say to you, you may not find their names in the Yellow Pages, but you will find them in the Lamb's Book of Life. They lived for God unknown to the world, and they died unknown to the world. But they are known to God, and their names are inscribed on high.

I had many things to write, but I will not with ink and pen write unto thee [3 John 13].

Though he wrote the Gospel of John and the Book of Revelation, two of the longest books of the New Testament, John very frankly says he would much rather tell it to you than write it to you.

> But I trust I shall shortly see thee, and we shall speak
> face to face. Peace be to thee. Our friends salute thee.
> Greet the friends by name [3 John 14].

Someday this will be true for you and me: we will be able to speak face
to face with John. I want to talk with him about these little books he
wrote. There are a lot of questions I want to ask him. But, of course,
he is referring to the fact that he will come and speak face to face with
these men of the first century. He will speak face to face with Diotrephes. I feel sorry for old Diotrephes—I'm sure he really got it in that
day. And John will speak to Gaius and Demetrius, those wonderful
men of God. He says, "We shall speak face to face."

"Peace be to thee. Our friends salute thee. Greet the friends by
name." Isn't that a lovely way to end this letter? John says, "I want you
to know that our friends who are here with me greet you. And will you
greet the friends by name? Go and say to Demetrius, 'Demetrius, I have
a message from John. He wanted to greet you and to tell you he will be
coming our way before long.'"

Gaius, Diotrephes, and Demetrius—these are the three men who
pass before us in this little epistle. Christianity was on trial in the first
century. Two of these men who are mentioned in this epistle are genuine. They are real and wonderful children of God. One is a delightful
brother; another is a dependable brother. But the third is a dictator and
a phony. May I say to you, the Gospel walked in shoe leather in the first
century in the Roman Empire. And it needs to get down where the
rubber meets the road in our day. In spite of any energy shortage, we
need to get the Gospel onto the highways and byways of life.

BIBLIOGRAPHY
(Recommended for Further Study)

Boice, James Montgomery. *The Epistles of John*. Grand Rapids, Michigan: Zondervan Publishing House, n.d.

Burdick, Donald W. *The Epistles of John*. Chicago, Illinois: Moody Press, 1970.

Ironside, H. A. *The Epistles of John*. Neptune, New Jersey: Loizeaux Brothers, 1931.

Kelly, William. *An Exposition of the Epistles of John*. Addison, Illinois: Bible Truth Publishers, 1905.

Mitchell, John G. *Fellowship: Three Letters From John*. Portland, Oregon: Multnomah Press, 1974.

Robertson, A. T. *Epochs in the Life of the Apostle John*. Grand Rapids, Michigan: Baker Book House, 1933.

Stott, J. R. W. *The Epistles of John*. Grand Rapids, Michigan: Wm. B. Eerdmans Publishing Co., 1964.

Strauss, Lehman. *The Epistles of John*. Neptune, New Jersey: Loizeaux Brothers, n.d.

Thomas, W. H. Griffith. *The Apostle John*. Grand Rapids, Michigan: Wm. B. Eerdmans Publishing Co., 1956.

Vaughan, Curtis. *1,2,3 John*. Grand Rapids, Michigan: Zondervan Publishing House, 1970.

Vine, W. E. *The Epistles of John*. Grand Rapids, Michigan: Zondervan Publishing House, n.d.

Wuest, Kenneth S. *In These Last Days*. Grand Rapids, Michigan: Wm. B. Eerdmans Publishing Co., 1954. (Deals with the epistles of 2 Peter, John, and Jude)

JUDE

The General Epistle of
JUDE
INTRODUCTION

Studying the little Epistle of Jude is like working a gold mine because of all the rich nuggets which are here just for the mining.

The writer is Jude, which is the English form of the name *Judas*. Jude, he tells us here, is the brother of James. Now, in the gospel records there are three or four men by the name of James, and there are three men by the name of Judas. We are helped in our identification of the writer of this epistle by the record in Matthew: "Is not this the carpenter's son? is not his mother called Mary? and his brethren, James, and Joses, and Simon, and Judas?" (Matt. 13:55). So two of these brothers, James, the writer of the Epistle of James, and Judas, the writer of the Epistle of Jude, are half brothers of the Lord Jesus Christ. There are two other men by the name of Judas, and they both were among the twelve apostles of our Lord. The best known, of course, is Judas Iscariot, the apostle who betrayed the Lord. The other apostle by the name of Judas is distinguished in this way: "Judas saith unto him, *not Iscariot*, Lord how is it that thou wilt manifest thyself unto us, and not unto the world?" (John 14:22, italics mine). The way he is identified is just that he is not Judas Iscariot. Therefore we believe that the writer of this epistle is the third Judas which Scripture mentions, Judas, the half brother of the Lord Jesus Christ.

Notice that neither James nor Jude identify themselves as brothers of the Lord Jesus. James introduces himself as ". . . a servant of God and of the Lord Jesus Christ . . ." (James 1:1). And Jude introduces himself as "the servant of Jesus Christ, and brother of James." Jude calls himself the servant, meaning "bond slave," of Jesus Christ. Why didn't James and Jude capitalize on their blood relationship with Jesus? I think the reason is obvious. Neither James nor Jude believed in the messianic claims of Jesus until *after* His resurrection. It was the Resurrection that convicted them and confirmed to them that Jesus was who He claimed to be. Up until that time they thought He had just gone "off" on religion, that He was, as the Scripture puts it, *beside Himself.* But after His resurrection they became believers. You see, it was possible to grow up in a home with Jesus in the days of His flesh and not recognize Him. I believe we see in Psalm 69 that He suffered loneliness and misunderstanding during those growing up years in Nazareth. Therefore His brothers felt that, although they had been reared with Him, they hadn't really *known* Him at that time. As Paul expressed it later, "Wherefore henceforth know we no man after the flesh: yea, though we have known Christ after the flesh, yet now henceforth know we him no more" (2 Cor. 5:16). Jude, though a half brother, recognizes that Jesus is the glorified Christ and that human relationship is not meaningful to him in any way. He had to come to Christ as a sinner, accepting Him as Savior just as anyone else did.

By the way, this is the marvelous answer of both James and Jude to an attitude which arose after the era of the apostles. There was a brief period when the family of Jesus was revered in a rather superstitious and sacred way as if they were something special. Actually, they were not superior; they were simply human beings who had to come to Christ just as you and I must come to Christ.

I have always felt that Protestantism has ignored Mary. She was a wonderful person. It was no accident that she was chosen of God to bear the Son of God, but that does not mean she is to be lifted up above all other people. She takes her own rightful place. Elizabeth called her blessed among women, not blessed above women, and Mary herself confessed her need of a Savior (see Luke 1:47). Therefore the brief period through which the church went when the family of the Lord Jesus was elevated to a very high position would certainly have been opposed by James and Jude. They themselves took the position of being merely bond slaves of Jesus Christ.

This book was written around A.D. 66–69.

The theme of the book is assurance in days of apostasy. Jude picked up the pen of inspiration to write on some theme or truth concerning the Gospel and our salvation. He could have chosen the subject of justification by faith, but Paul had written on that in Romans. He could have chosen the resurrection of Christ, but Paul had written on that in 1 Corinthians. Or he could have chosen the doctrine of reconciliation, but Paul had written on that in 2 Corinthians. Probably Jude could have written on the great subject of faith, but Paul had written on that in Galatians. Or he could have selected the church as the body of Christ, but Paul had written on that in Ephesians. Or he could have selected the person of Christ, but Paul had written on that in Colossians. Jude could have written about our Great High Priest, but the writer to the Hebrews had already written on that. Or he could have chosen the subject of fellowship, but John was going to write on that later on. So the Spirit of God caused him to develop another subject rather than to develop one of the great doctrines. The Spirit of God arrested his purpose before he could even put down his subject and directed him into another channel. Jude's subject is the coming apostasy. He gives us the most vivid account that we have of the apostasy, and he presents it in a very dramatic manner. Jude hangs out a red lantern on the most dangerous curve along the highway the church of Christ is traveling. Jude describes in vivid terms and with awe-inspiring language the frightful conditions that were coming in the future. This little epistle is like a burglar alarm. Apostates have broken into the church. They came in the side door while nobody was watching. And this little epistle is like an atom bomb. The first bomb did not fall on Hiroshima or Nagasaki; it fell when Jude wrote this little epistle. It's an atom bomb, and it exploded in the early church as a warning.

Jude gives the only record in Scripture regarding the contention of Satan with Michael the archangel over the body of Moses. It is a very remarkable passage of Scripture.

Also, Jude records the prophecy of Enoch, which is found nowhere else in Scripture. He sees the Lord coming with ten thousands of His saints.

The little prophecy of Jude affords a fitting introduction to the Book of Revelation.

OUTLINE

I. **Occasion of the Epistle, Verses 1–3**
   A. Assurance for Believers, Verses 1–2
      (Sanctified, kept, called)
   B. Change of Theme to Apostasy, Verse 3

II. **Occurrences of Apostasy, Verses 4–16**
   A. Inception of Apostasy, Verse 4
   B. Israel in Unbelief Destroyed in Wilderness, Verse 5
   C. Angels Rebelled; Kept in Chains, Verse 6
   D. Sodom and Gomorrah Sinned in Sexuality; Destroyed by Fire, Verse 7
   E. Modern Apostate Teachers Identified, Verses 8–10
      (Despise authority)
   F. Cain, Balaam, Korah—Examples of Apostates, Verse 11
   G. Modern Apostate Teachers Defined and Described, Verses 12–16

III. **Occupation of Believers in Days of Apostasy, Verses 17–25**
   A. Believers Warned by Apostles That These Apostates Would Come, Verses 17–19
   B. What Believers Must Do in Days of Apostasy, Verses 20–25
      1. Build Up
      2. Pray In
      3. Keep Themselves
      4. Look For
      5. Have Compassion
      6. Save Others
      7. Hate Evil

JUDE

OCCASION OF THE EPISTLE

In the first three verses, Jude gives the occasion for his writing this epistle. Jude will tell us that he intended to write on some theme of our salvation, but the Spirit of God put up a red warning sign and instructed him to call attention to the days of apostasy which would be coming upon the church.

ASSURANCE FOR BELIEVERS

Jude, the servant of Jesus Christ, and brother of James, to them that are sanctified by God the Father, and preserved in Jesus Christ, and called [Jude 1].

"Jude" as I pointed out in the Introduction, is the English form of the name Judas. in the New Testament, there are three men who bear the name Judas, but we have very good evidence which identifies the writer of this epistle as the half brother of the Lord Jesus Christ.

"The servant of Jesus Christ." The word servant is literally "bond slave." He claims no blood relationship with the Lord Jesus as if that would give him a superior position. This ought to lay to rest the notion which arose in the early church, in the post-apostolic period, that the family of Jesus was to be held in reverence because they were super-duper folk. Dr. Marvin R. Vincent, the outstanding Greek scholar, comments in *Word Studies in the New Testament*:

That Jude does not allude to his relationship to the Lord may be explained by the fact that the natural relationship in his mind would be subordinate to the spiritual (see Luke xi. 27, 28), and that such a designation would, as Dean Alford remarks, "have been in harmony with those later and superstitious feelings with which the next and following ages regarded the Lord's earthly relatives."

"The brother of James," as we have said in the Introduction, is the way Jude identifies himself. Both James and Jude were half brothers of the Lord Jesus, and James was the writer of the epistle which bears his name. He was mentioned by the apostle Paul as one of the pillars in the church at Jerusalem.

"To them that are sanctifed by God the father." The Greek text of Nestle and that of Westcott and Hort, which are the best Greek texts that we have, use the verb *agapaō*, meaning "to love," instead of *hagiazō*, meaning "to sanctify." Most scholars agree that "to love" is more accurate than "to sanctify," and it makes it a little bit more precious to our hearts to know that we are loved or beloved by God the Father.

I would like to share with you the translation of Kenneth S. Wuest, the late Greek scholar at the Moody Bible Institute. His translation (*Word Studies from the Greek New Testament*), though a bit involved, in many places brings out the original meaning:

Jude, a bondslave of Jesus Christ and brother of James, to those who by God the Father have been loved and are in a state of being the permanent objects of His love, and who for Jesus Christ have been guarded and are in a permanent state of being carefully watched, to those who are called ones.

This is a wonderful passage of Scripture. We are beloved by God the Father and preserved for Jesus Christ.

There are several words I must deal with in this text because of their importance. The first word is *preserved*. It is this word that gives us the key to the Book of Jude which presents the apostasy as it is presented nowhere else in Scripture. How frightful it is! But Jude doesn't write just to frighten the daylights out of us. Nor does he write just to draw a vivid picture for our information; he gives us this background in order that he might give *assurance* in days of apostasy. He uses the word *keep* four times, which is what the word preserve means. They are kept in Jesus Christ—God is the one who keeps them. Notice verse 21 says "keep yourselves in the love of God"; and verse 24 says "now unto him that is able to *keep* you from falling." You may call it anything you want to, but it gives assurance of salvation to the believer even in the dark days of apostasy.

As we shall see, you and I are presently living in the apostasy. How much farther we will go into it before the Rapture, I do not know—nor does anyone else know. But we definitely are in times of apostasy.

Now looking again at the word *preserved*, it is interesting to note that in the physical world there are two ways of preserving food. One is with vinegar, and the other is with sugar. There are many saints in our day who I think are preserved all right, but they are preserved in vinegar—that is, they act that way. They have a vinegar disposition. Also, there are saints who are preserved in sugar. They are sugar and spice and everything nice—and these are not all women either. But even those who seem to be preserved in vinegar are preserved by God's grace, which preserves or keeps them. The apostle John will tell us in Revelation 12:11 that ". . . they overcame him [Satan] by the blood of the Lamb . . .", and that is the only way believers are going to make it through the Great Tribulation. And that is the only way *we* are going to overcome—by the blood of the Lamb. There is no merit or power in us to overcome the Evil One.

I must resort back to the illustration which the Lord Jesus Himself gave when He said, "I am the good shepherd: the good shepherd giveth his life for the sheep" (John 10:11). Then He goes on to talk about His sheep, "My sheep hear my voice, and I know them, and they follow me: And I give unto them eternal life; and they shall never perish, neither shall any man pluck them out of my hand. My Father, which gave them me, is greater than all; and no man is able to pluck them out of my Father's hand" (John 10:27–29).

Now if a sheep is kept in safety, it is no credit to the sheep. A sheep cannot defend itself. It doesn't have sharp fangs and claws to fight its enemy. Neither can it run. A jackrabbit can't defend itself either, but a jackrabbit can get away from trouble. A sheep can't even do that. A sheep is helpless. When one of God's sheep says that he knows he is saved, he is not boasting of his own merit; he is boasting of his Shepherd. He has a wonderful Shepherd. My friend, if you are saying that you are not sure of your salvation, you really are reflecting upon your Shepherd, because He says that He can keep you. He says that no created thing is able to take you out of His Father's hand. It is not a question of whether or not you can hold on to Him. It is a question of His holding on to you. He says that He can, and it is a matter of your trusting Him.

You see, salvation rests upon the Word of God. It is up to you whether you will believe Him or not. Your assurance of salvation rests upon that because He has made it very clear that you have a sure salvation. Here in Jude we are presented with the dark days of apostasy, and God still says that He is able to keep His own.

"And called." Not only are we preserved in Jesus Christ, safe in Him, but we are also called. The word *called*, as it is used in Scripture, is not only an invitation that is sent out, but it is an invitation that is sent out and accepted and made real because of the Spirit of God. Let me give you Paul's statement as found in 1 Corinthians 1:22–24: "For the Jews require a sign, and the Greeks seek after wisdom: But we preach Christ crucified, unto the Jews a stumblingblock, and unto the Greeks foolishness; But unto them which are *called*, both Jews and Greeks, Christ the power of God, and the wisdom of God" (italics mine). My friend, if you have found in Christ the wisdom and power of God and you have trusted Him, you are one of "the called." The invitation is sent out, and when it is accepted and believed, then you are the called. That is exactly what Jude means here, and Paul spelled it out for us as well.

Mercy unto you, and peace, and love, be multiplied [Jude 2].

We need to recognize the difference between these three words: mercy, peace, and love; then we need to see the strong relationship between them.

Love is an attribute of God. Because God is love, He is merciful and has provided grace. The love of God encompasses all mankind—"God

For in such a manner does

so loved the *world*" (see John 3:16) It is not His will that any [the Elect] should perish. Today He loves every [Elect] human being on this earth. He has no favorites. Way back in the Book of Exodus, God made it clear to even a man like Moses that He did not answer his prayer because he was Moses; "And he said, I . . . will be gracious to whom I will be gracious, and will shew mercy on whom I will shew mercy" (Exod. 33:19). God answered Moses' prayer because He found the explanation in Himself; He treats all His creatures alike in that sense. My friend, God loves you today. If you knew how much He loves you, it would break your heart—you would be in tears.

Now you can keep from experiencing God's love, but you cannot keep Him from loving you. You can't keep the sun from shining, but you can put up an umbrella to keep the sun from shining on you. And there are certain umbrellas you can put up to keep from experiencing the love of God: the umbrella of resistance to His will, the umbrella of sin in your life, etc.

Although God loved you, He did not save you by love. You see, God has other attributes. He is holy. He is righteous. He is just. He simply cannot let down the bars of heaven and, by lowering His standards, bring you in. He cannot do that any more than a human judge can uphold the laws of the land and yet accept a bribe under the table for letting a criminal off. If he does that, he is a crooked judge. And if God is going to do that with human beings, He is no better than a crooked judge. I do not mean to be irreverent because God is not a crooked judge. God has to maintain His holiness and His righteousness and His justice.

"God so loved the world," and He loved the world with a merciful love, a love that had a concern and care for human beings. And because of it, He gave His only begotten Son—He provided His Son as the substitute. Now God, on a righteous basis, can save a sinner if he will come to Him and accept His salvation. This is called the *grace* of God. "For by grace are ye saved through faith; and that not of yourselves: it is the gift of God: Not of works, lest any man should boast" (Eph. 2:8–9).

In *Synonyms of the New Testament* Dr. R. C. Trench, who was a great Greek scholar, made a clear distinction between these words:

> While *charis* [grace] has thus reference to the *sins* of men, and is that glorious attribute of God which these sins call out and display, His *free gift* in their forgiveness, *eleos* [mercy], has special and immediate regard to the *misery* which is the consequence of these sins.

Now you can see that the *grace* of God, not the love of God, has to do with the sins of men. God has provided a Savior who has paid the penalty for sins. On that basis, God saves sinners. That is the grace of God.

However, sin has brought tragedy to the human family. We often hear the question: Why does a God of love permit cancer? Well, disease and death came to the human family as consequences of sin. God sees the misery that sin has caused, and the mercy of God goes out to man. God is rich in mercy. If you come to Him as a sinner and accept His salvation, He will save you by grace. Then, because He is rich in mercy, He will extend His mercy to you. He will bring comfort to you at that time. He will help you and comfort your heart. You can trust Him in your time of need.

The fellow who is writing these words has had two major operations for cancer, and the doctors tell me the cancer is still in my body and can break out anytime. To be frank with you, from where I sit right now I have a great big question: Why? And I am asking the Lord why. But my only refuge is in my heavenly Father. I know He has the answer, although He hasn't told me what it is. What I'm asking from Him is mercy. He has already saved me by His grace, but now I want His mercy. Mercy is that love of His which goes out to us in our misery here upon this earth.

A sinner needs the grace of God, and he sure needs a whole lot of mercy—I've been using a great deal of it these past few years.

Let me share with you from Dr. Trench again. I will repeat what I have already quoted and then go on:

> While *charis* has thus reference to the *sins* of men, and is that glorious attribute of God which these sins call out and display, His *free gift* in their forgiveness, *eleos*, has special and immediate regard to the *misery* which is the consequence of these sins,

being the tender sense of this misery displaying itself in the effort, which only the continued perverseness of man can hinder or defeat, to assuage and entirely remove it. . . . In the divine mind, and in the order of our salvation as conceived therein, the *eleos* (mercy) precedes the *charis* (grace). God so loved the world with a pitying love (herein was the *eleos*), that He gave His only begotten Son (herein the *charis*), that the world through Him might be saved (compare Eph. 2:4; Luke 1:78–79). But in the order of the manifestation of God's purposes of salvation the grace must go before the mercy, the *charis* must go before and make way for the *eleos*. It is true that the same persons are the subjects of both, being at once the guilty and the miserable; yet the righteousness of God, which it is quite necessary should be maintained as His love, demands that the guilt should be done away before the misery can be assuaged; only the forgiven can be blessed.

God must pardon before He can heal. Men must be justified before they can be sanctified. In the order of the manifestation of God's purposes of salvation, the grace of God must go before the mercy of God. The grace must go before and take away and make way for the mercy of God.

The "peace" of God is that experience which comes to the heart that is trusting Christ. Paul says, "Therefore being justified by faith, we have *peace* with God through our Lord Jesus Christ" (Rom. 5:1, italics mine). Peace with God is to know that God is not difficult to get along with. He is not making it hard for me; He is not making it hard for you. He wants us to know that He hasn't anything against us now that we know that we are sinners and have trusted Christ as our Savior. The world may point its finger at you and reject you, but God has accepted you. He loves you, and He wants to give you that peace so that at night you can pillow your head on God's promises. "And we know that all things work together for good to them that love God, to them who are the called according to his purpose" (Rom 8:28) Dr R. A. Terrey used to call this verse a soft pillow for a tired heart. What a wonderful promise it is!

CHANGE OF THEME TO APOSTASY

Beloved, when I gave all diligence to write unto you of
the common salvation, it was needful for me to write
unto you, and exhort you that ye should earnestly contend for the faith which was once delivered unto the
saints [Jude 3].

"Beloved." When Jude uses that term, it really means folk who are
loved of God, God's beloved children.

"Common salvation." Let's understand that the word *common* is
the English translation of the Greek word *koinēs*. The New Testament
was not written in classical Greek but in *koinē* Greek or common
Greek, meaning that it was understood by everyone, educated and un-
educated, all over the Roman Empire in the days of the apostles. When
Jude said that he had intended to write of the "common salvation," he
must have been referring to something that people throughout the Roman Empire would understand.

Now Jude says here that he was planning on writing on some facet
of our salvation. It could have been on redemption, on the person of
Christ, on sanctification, or any number of themes, but he didn't write
on any of those themes because "it was needful for me to write unto
you, and exhort you that ye should earnestly contend for the faith
which was once delivered unto the saints." The thought here is that the
Holy Spirit detoured Jude from writing on some theme of the faith in
order that he might sound a warning concerning the impending apostasy.

The apostasy is a departure from the faith, that is, from the apostles' doctrine. Apostasy was just a little cloud the size of a man's hand
in Jude's day, but now it is a storm of hurricane force that fills the land.
As Jude writes about the apostasy that was coming on the earth, we
can see that many of the things he mentions are already taking place in
the world in our day. My friend, the apostasy is not something *we* are
looking forward to; the apostasy is here. It is all about us today.

"Needful." There was a compulsion, a necessity, a constraint upon

Jude. He said, "When I was about to write to you about some great doctrine which the apostles gave us, a necessity was laid upon me instead to exhort you that you should earnestly contend for the faith."

"Contend." There are expositors who suggest that this means to contend on your knees. Well, I have never been able to find any authority for that view, but the thought here is to contend without being contentious. I wish we fundamentalists could contend for the fundamentals of the faith without being fiery and contentious. As Paul put it, "And the servant of the Lord must not strive; but be gentle unto all men, apt [ready] to teach, patient, In meekness instructing those that oppose themselves; if God peradventure will give them repentance to the acknowledging of the truth; And that they may recover themselves out of the snare of the devil, who are taken captive by him at his will" (2 Tim. 2:24–26). The word *contend*, as Jude uses it, has in it the idea of agony. The Greek word is *epagōnizesthai*, and we get our English word *agony* from the noun of this word. Instead of writing on some great doctrine, Jude is saying that we are to contend or defend the great doctrines of Christianity.

"Contend for the faith which was once delivered unto the saints." "The faith" was the body of truth given once for all. In the Book of Acts it is called the apostles' doctrine: "And they continued stedfastly in the apostles' doctrine and fellowship, and in breaking of bread, and in prayers" (Acts 2:42). Notice that the apostles' doctrine is the first thing mentioned. Since that is number one on God's church parade, our church is not a church unless it is doing just that.

We are told in Ephesians 4:15 to speak the truth in love or, as someone has translated it, "truthing in love." My friend if you are going to give out the truth, give it out in love. If you do not give it out in love, there is some question about whether or not you are actually giving out the truth. And we are to be ready to give an answer to anyone who asks us—in meekness and fear. A believer should not have a short fuse and become angry when someone differs with him.

Dr. Kenneth S. Wuest has one of the finest books available which gives the literal translation of Jude. Notice his translation in *Word Studies from the Greek New Testament*:

Divinely-loved ones, when giving all diligence to be writing to you concerning the salvation possessed in common by all of us, I had constraint laid upon me to write to you, beseeching (you) to contend with intensity and determination for the Faith once for all entrusted into the safekeeping of the saints.

OCCURRENCES OF APOSTASY

Now Jude will set before us the reason we should contend for the faith. Something is happening to the church, and Jude sounds an alarm.

INCEPTION OF APOSTASY

For there are certain men crept in unawares, who were before of old ordained to this condemnation, ungodly men, turning the grace of our God into lasciviousness, and denying the only Lord God, and our Lord Jesus Christ [Jude 4].

"Who were before of old ordained to this condemnation" should be made clear first of all. It actually means that they were written of beforehand. The word ordained is prographō, meaning "to write beforehand." It simply means that other writers had sounded the warning about apostates.

"There are certain men crept in unawares"—they are creeps! Crept in is one of the most interesting phrases in the Greek language. It is pareisdunō. Dunō means "to enter"; the preposition eis means "into"; and para means "beside." It means "to enter alongside" or, as Dr. Vincent puts it in his commentary: "To get in by the side, to slip in a side door." This is the way the apostates have come into the church.

I have been in the church for many years. I have been and am still an ordained Presbyterian preacher—although I am in no denomination today and have no denominational connections at all. As a young person I remember that the church was by and large sound in the faith. When I went to the denominational college, I began to discover that there were ministers who denied practically every tenet of the faith. That opened up a new world to me. Then when I went to the denominational seminary, I found that the liberal element was still growing. The day came when I left that denomination and came to California. Here I entered another denomination, and when I saw it going into liberalism, I got out. I wasn't put out; I just stepped out voluntarily. During that long period I saw how these men were able to take over a church. They came in the side door. They came in by professing one thing and believing another. They did not come in the front door—that is, they did not declare their doctrinal position. Many of our good laymen have been deceived by ministers like that. Scripture has warned about them. For instance, Paul wrote to the Corinthians: "For such are false apostles, deceitful workers, transforming themselves into the apostles of Christ. And no marvel; for Satan himself is transformed into an angel of light. Therefore it is no great thing if his ministers also be transformed as the ministers of righteousness; whose end shall be according to their works" (2 Cor. 11:13–15). The expression "transforming themselves" in this verse is very interesting. It is in the Greek *metaschōmatixontai*, meaning "the act of an individual who is changing his outward expression by *assuming* an expression put on from the outside." It is a method of Satan.

Over the years I have seen as many as a dozen strong, outstanding churches across America fall into the hands of liberalism by this method. It is the most deceitful method in the world. Let me give you an instance of one church. I won't give the location, because the chances are that you know one like it in the area in which you live. It was, at one time, a church in which the Word of God was preached, people were being saved, and hearts were being blessed. Then the pastor retired or resigned, and a new man appeared on the scene. When he met with the pulpit committee and met with the elders, they asked him about his doctrinal beliefs. He assured them that he believed in all the great doctrines of the faith. You see, he came in the side door because he really did not believe them. He only pretended to believe them and pretended to be sound in the faith. And the interesting thing is that his trial sermon sounded as though he were sound in the faith. He had probably read Spurgeon or Warfield or G. Campbell Morgan and had borrowed enough of their material to preach a good sermon. Hearing him, the congregation thought, *This young man is just fine;* so they called him as their pastor. But remember that he came in by the side door; he did not believe the doctrine that he preached. Before long they discovered that they had a liberal on their hands. Generally, fundamental churches consider ousting the preacher to be a bad method; so they tolerate him. However, my feeling is that since he came in by the side door, he should be booted out the back door. But they don't do that. Right at this moment I know of two or three churches which are being ruined by men who pretended to be what they were not.

Remember that Jude said that they "were before of old ordained to this condemnation"—that is, they were written of beforehand. Jude is saying, "I'm not telling you something new—others have written of this also and have warned you of that which is coming."

Paul is one who repeatedly warned of the apostate. The last time he went by Ephesus, at his last visit with the Ephesian elders, he gave this warning: "For I know this, that after my departing shall grievous wolves enter in among you, not sparing the flock. Also of your own selves shall men arise, speaking perverse things, to draw away disciples after them. Therefore watch, and remember, that by the space of three years I ceased not to warn every one night and day with tears" (Acts 20:29–31). Although Paul warned them of apostates, the day came when the Ephesian church yielded to them.

Paul also warned the young preacher Timothy: "Having a form of godliness, but denying the power thereof: from such turn away. For of this sort are they which creep into houses, and lead captive silly women laden with sins, led away with divers lusts" (2 Tim. 3:5–6). One of the greatest movements we have seen in our day is the formation of women's Bible study classes all across this country. I thank God for them. However, it needs to be watched very carefully because, since it is a success, you will find that somebody is going to try the side door and slip in. In the history of the church there has never been a woman theologian, and that is very strange indeed. Also, it is true that women have played a prominent part in many of the cults and heresies that have come into the church. While I don't claim to be an authority in this field, it seems to me that a woman is built finer than a man. She has finer sensibilities and a closer perception than a man has. For this reason she needs to be treated with more care. I have to be more particular with my watch than I have to be with the motor in my car. There is a grave danger (and I have heard this voiced by several ministers across the country) of these women's movements operating totally outside the church and not cooperating with the church at all. This is also true of the youth movement which is taking place. Also, I have found in my radio ministry that I move largely outside the local church. However, I do try to work with the local church, and I believe that all of these movements should work with the local church if it is a Bible-believing church. Paul is warning about false teachers coming in the side door, and I believe that any movement today which the Spirit of God seems to be blessing needs to be watched very carefully because of the fact that the Devil is going to come in the side door if he can. And if you think he is coming in as the *Devil*, you are wrong. His ministers pretend to be ministers of light.

The final test, the acid test, of any movement is the teaching regarding the person of Jesus Christ. If it denies the deity of Christ, you can rule it out immediately, but you have to be very careful about this matter of the deity of Christ. There are many facets by which they can deny the deity of Christ and yet give the impression that they actually believe in Him as the Savior of the world. Simon Peter warns of this: "But there were false prophets also among the people, even as there shall be false teachers among you, who privily shall bring in damnable heresies, even denying the Lord that bought them, and bring upon themselves swift destruction" (2 Pet. 2:1).

And Paul, writing to the Galatians, warns: "And that because of false brethren unawares brought in, who came in privily to spy out our liberty which we have in Christ Jesus, that they might bring us into bondage" (Gal. 2:4). My friend, we need to guard every movement today which God is blessing. These organizations which are outside the church may go off on tangents because the ministers of Satan are waiting to come in the side door. "Ungodly men turning the grace of our God into lasciviousness, and denying the only Lord God, and our Lord Jesus Christ." They are by nature ungodly men, and they do two things: (1) They distort and deny the grace of God—"turning the grace of our God into lasciviousness"; and (2) they deny the deity of the Lord Jesus Christ—"denying the only Lord God, and our Lord Jesus Christ."

"Ungodly" means that they simply leave God out of their lives.

It is important to evaluate whether or not a man who teaches and preaches the Word of God is a godly man. I was amazed to hear from a couple who, I thought, had good spiritual discernment. They attended the classes of a Bible teacher and were greatly impressed by him. In fact, they considered him outstanding. They were willing to tolerate the fact that this Bible teacher was having an open affair with a woman who was not his wife! A man may be an interesting Bible teacher and still be an ungodly man. We need to look at their lives. Are they leaving God out of their lives?

Lasciviousness is a very important word. I suppose the best synonym is *wantonness* because wantonness has in it the thought of lawlessness and arrogance—doing as you please even if you offend the sensibilities of others. Jude says that the ungodly turn the grace of our God into lasciviousness—into immorality. The apostle Paul warned the Galatian believers about the danger of turning the grace of God into license—permitting them to live any way they pleased. "For, brethren, ye have been called unto liberty; only use not liberty for an occasion to the flesh, but by love serve one another" (Gal. 5:13).

Gross immorality characterizes the apostasy of our day. They have thrown overboard all of the great precepts of Scripture concerning morality, and they call it the new morality. There is a growing danger in this country of the church actually espousing and condoning gross immorality. One writer has said that "one of the troubles with the world is that people mistake sex for love, money for brains, and transistor radios for civilization." The creed of the present day, according to the late Dr. Wallace Petty, can be stated in the following six articles: "God is a creation of wishful thinking; religion is a mechanism of escape from reality; man is a glorified gorilla who asks too many questions and represses too many desires; morals are a matter of taste; love is an art; and life is a racket." That is the viewpoint of some folk in our day.

The wantonness that we are seeing is marked by an arrogant recklessness of justice. Another definition is "willfully malicious." Marriage is flouted and considered unessential. You may live with whomever you wish to live with in total disregard of the morality which builds homes and thereby builds a nation. As far back as 1959 Vice Admiral Robert Goldthwaite, Chief of Naval Air Training, told a large group of leading educators, businessmen, law enforcement officials, and others that there is "a surge of immorality in civilian and military life." He said that "moral decay" is an acute national problem, and there is urgent need to improve "moral leadership" among youth. During the years since then, the moral decay has reached such proportions that we should be alarmed. We ought to be very careful about the folk who are teaching in our churches. Are they teaching a loose morality? Jude warns us to be on our guard against that.

The other thing that characterizes an apostate is that he denies the Lord God and our Lord Jesus Christ. He will talk about God and the Lord Jesus, but he denies who and what they actually are.

In Jude's day the apostasy was Gnosticism. Gnosticism taught that the body was essentially evil, that all matter was evil, and that the spirit alone was good. The conclusion drawn from this was that it didn't matter what a man did with his body. He was free to satisfy the lusts of the body. He was free to practice blatant immorality, shameless sin, and arrogantly and proudly to flout that sin publicly. That was a perversion of grace.

The same ideas have sprung up again today. The new morality is no newer than the old Gnosticism, the first heresy. The other facet of Gnosticism was a denial of the true God and true Man, our Lord Jesus Christ. That is the mark of an antichrist. John calls such people antichrists in his epistle. It is always the spirit of antichrist which denies the Lord Jesus Christ.

I have spent a long time on this verse because of the importance of the matters it sets before us.

ISRAEL IN UNBELIEF DESTROYED
IN THE WILDERNESS

Now Jude is going to give us six examples of apostasy in the past. Before we look at this section, let me remind you of what the apostasy is. Thayer gives this meaning for the Greek word *aphistēmi:* "to remove, to withdraw, to go away, to depart." When the word is used in 2 Thessalonians, I take the position that it has a twofold meaning. It means the removal of the church since in Paul's first epistle to the Thessalonians he spoke of the rapture of the church. The Rapture must come first—the *aphistēmi,* the departure, the removal of the church. The removal of believers from the earth will lead to the total apostasy—that is, the departure from the faith. Our Lord Jesus asked the question, ". . . when the Son of man cometh [to the earth], shall he find [the] faith . . . ?" (Luke 18:8). The way the question is couched in the Greek demands a negative answer. Therefore, the answer is no, He will not find the faith on the earth when He returns. There will be a total departure, a total apostasy. Now that cannot come about until the true believers are removed from the earth—and, of course, this can occur at any moment.

Jude is now going to give us six examples of apostasy in the past; that is, departures from the faith. There will be three groups and then three individuals. First, the three groups—

I will therefore put you in remembrance, though ye once knew this, how that the Lord, having saved the people out of the land of Egypt, afterward destroyed them that believed not [Jude 5].

In the wilderness, Israel in unbelief was destroyed, and it is an example that God does judge apostates. When Israel came to Kadesh-Barnea, they refused to enter the Promised Land.

Now the spies had brought back a report to Kadesh-Barnea that everything God had told them about the land was accurate. But the spies (with the exception of two) didn't believe that God could bring them into the land, and they persuaded the people to believe that. At first they didn't want to believe that it was a good land. After they were convinced it was a good land, they wouldn't believe that God could bring them into the land. They preferred to stay in the wilderness rather than believe God. That is an example of apostasy, a departure from the faith. They departed from the whole basis on which they had left Egypt. God had given them a promise with two parts to it: "I will take you out of Egypt and I will bring you into the land." But Israel's unbelief pushed them back into the wilderness, and God left them there for thirty-eight more years until all of the adult generation had died—with the exception of Caleb and Joshua. Israel had used their children as an excuse for not going into the land; so God said, "But your little ones, which ye said should be a prey, them will I bring in, and they shall know the land which ye have despised" (Num. 14:31).

My friend, in our own lives we sometimes use our children's welfare as an excuse for not serving the Lord. While that sounds very noble, it infers that God isn't thinking of our children. God will take care of them and us when we obey Him.

The new generation of Israel did cross the Jordan River and enter the Promised Land, even as God had promised. However, the generation that had apostatized, that had departed from the faith, were destroyed in the wilderness, and they are the first example that Jude gives.

ANGELS IN REBELLION KEPT IN CHAINS

And the angels which kept not their first estate, but left their own habitation, he hath reserved in everlasting chains under darkness unto the judgment of the great day [Jude 6].

This opens up to us a truth that we don't get with such clarity in any other section of the Word of God, although we are told that there will be a judgment of angels. Sometime in the past they didn't keep "their first estate." God created angels with a free will. Angels do not reproduce as human beings do; therefore, they do not inherit a sinful nature as humans do. Each angel is created by God with a free will. Now, some of these spiritual creatures were caught up in a rebellion, and now they are reserved in chains.

Apparently, the fallen angels are divided into two groups. The group whose rebellion was so great is evidently locked up, incarcerated, and has no freedom of movement any longer. The other group of fallen angels apparently has freedom of movement and is under the leadership of Satan. It seems evident that these are the demons mentioned in Scripture and that are coming into prominence in our day.

For many years the liberal wing of the church has denied the supernatural and denied that there were any such creatures as angels. We are living in a materialistic age, and the viewpoint was that God and the idea of angels were superstitions that we no longer needed. I believe it was Huxley who said that the belief in God was like the fading smile of a Cheshire cat, that it was disappearing in this scientific age.

Back in 1963 Ben Hecht wrote an article under the title, "New God for the Space Age." Let me quote the first few paragraphs:

> The most amazing event to enter modern history has been generally snubbed by our chroniclers. It is the petering out of Christianity. Not only are the Bible stories going by the board, but a deeper side of religion seems also to be exiting. This is the mystic concept of the human soul and its survival after death.
>
> Parsons are still preaching away on this topic and congregations are still listening. But congregation and parson both seem to have moved from church to museum.
>
> Fifty years ago religion was an exuberant part of our world. Its sermons, bazaars, tag days, taboos and exhortations filled the press. Its rituals brought a glow to our citizenry. At their supper tables a large part of the voting population bowed its head and said grace.
>
> Religion today is a touchy subject, not because people believe deeply and are ready to defend such belief with emotion, but because they do not want to hear it discussed. They do not know quite what they feel and they do not know what to say about God, His angels and the record of His miracles. Not wanting to sound anti-Christian (or antisocial or anti-anything not under general condemnation) they settle for silence. In this silence, more than in all the previous agnostic hullabaloos, religion seems swiftly disappearing.

Remember that Ben Hecht wrote that in 1963. Since that time there has been a tremendous revival.

For many years liberalism has been predicting the death knell of the church and of all that is supernatural. Around 1963 Gibson Winter, a professor of ethics at the University of Chicago Divinity School, wrote a book entitled *The Suburban Captivity of the Churches* in which he made this statement:

> U.S. Protestantism—once famous for its diversity—is homogenizing into what is almost a new faith, and if it continues in its present direction, it will be stone-cold dead in a couple of dozen years.

I could give you quotations *ad nauseam* of what liberals said a few years ago. For instance, a man at the Chicago Theological Seminary made the statement that Protestantism has gotten so prosperous statistically that it has lost all internal discipline whatsoever. "It looks frightfully confining from the outside, but on the inside it has no discipline, no integrity."

These quotations give a picture of the contemporary liberal church.

However, more recently there has been a revival of interest in that which is supernatural. It is quite interesting that the revival did not come from within the church, not even from within the fundamental church. It came on the campuses of the colleges, especially the campuses of some colleges which a few years ago were totally materialistic and denied everything of the supernatural. Today they are talking about demonism, about Satan, and actually about God and the Bible. All of a sudden an interest in the supernatural has appeared again, and angels seem to make sense even in the space age.

Men and women are concerned as they look about at a world of materialism that has gone crazy. We know how to get to the moon, but we do not know how to control human nature here on this earth. A great problem is arising right here in Southern California. A reputable paper has come out with the fact that Los Angeles is becoming an armed city with gangs who roam the streets. They are free to roam the streets while law-abiding people are imprisoned in their homes, afraid to venture out. Los Angeles has become an armed camp.

A few years ago this materialistic generation was saying that human nature was getting better, and since it has been improved, we don't need all of our laws; so the lid was taken off. My friend, we found out that instead of its being a bucket of rosewater, it was a bucket of stinking garbage! Vile and unspeakable crimes have been committed; unbelievable immorality has taken place. The question is being asked, "Where does all this vileness and evil come from?" As someone has expressed it, "If there were not the Devil, men would have to invent a devil to explain all the evil which is in this world today."

It really is not possible to deny that humanity is depraved. None of us seems to realize fully that we belong to a race that is totally depraved and that we live in a world that is under the control of Satan. It was thought that the removal of laws and restrictions would produce a wonderful, free society. However, the developments of recent years have caused men to return to the supernatural. Unfortunately, the emphasis has been on the evil spirits. Men have found they must believe in the evil spirits to explain the wickedness they find in the world.

Well, the Bible has something to say about it. My friend, the Bible is very much up to date. It is the Bible that tells us about the angels which rebelled against God and about those whom "he hath reserved in everlasting chains under darkness unto the judgment of the great day."

The Word of God has a great deal to say about the judgments that are coming. Folk without a knowledge of the Bible speak of one great judgment day which is coming. Well, the Great White Throne judgment is coming in the future for the unsaved (see Rev. 20:11-15), but actually there are eight judgments mentioned in the Word of God. One of those eight judgments is the judgment of angels, which will take place during the last days.

In 1 Corinthians we are told the order of the resurrections— ". . . Christ the firstfruits; afterward they that are Christ's at his coming. Then cometh the end, when he shall have delivered up the kingdom to God, even the Father; when he shall have put down all rule and all authority and power. [The power is obviously evil power, the demonic forces which are in the world.] For he must reign, till he hath put all enemies under his feet" (1 Cor. 15:23-25). So during the Millennium these demonic powers will be judged.

The Scriptures have a great deal to say about the judgment of angels. Let me cite another passage: "Know ye not that we shall judge angels? how much more things that pertain to this life?" (1 Cor. 6:3). This is something that we would not have known if Paul hadn't mentioned it. We will be with our Lord during the Millennium. (We'll probably commute back and forth from earth to the New Jerusalem which is the eternal home of the church.) And at some period, probably during that thousand-year reign of Christ on the earth, there will be the judgment of angels. Although we were created lower than the angels, someday we will have part in their judgment.

Peter gives another reference to the judgment of angels which corresponds to that of Jude: "For if God spared not the angels that sinned, but cast them down to hell [hades, the place of the unsaved dead], and delivered them into chains of darkness, to be reserved unto judgment" (2 Pet. 2:4). "Chains of darkness" could not refer to our conception of chains as a series of connected metal links, because angels are spiritual creatures and it would be pretty difficult to put a physical chain on them! The word *chains* means "bonds," indicating that they are heavily guarded in a certain place. Again I turn to Dr. Wuest's translation:

And angels who did not carefully guard their original position of preeminent dignity, but abandoned once for all their own private dwelling-place, with a view to the judgment of the great day, in everlasting bonds under darkness, He has put under careful guard.

As we have seen, this company of angels is awaiting the judgment which apparently will come during the last days.

The other group of fallen angels are the demons which are abroad in the world today. Demonic power, of course, is a reality, although I personally feel that it is being overplayed at the time I am writing this. There is probably a good percentage of so-called demon activity that is phony, but certainly some of it is impossible to explain as natural phenomena. This is the reason the movie, *The Exorcist*, got under the skin of so many people. Although some of it was fictional, it was based on a factual case. It is an example of the forces of evil that are in the world. It actually took place, and there are other cases like it.

The Book of Revelation has several references to the judgment of fallen angels. "And the devil that deceived them was cast into the lake of fire and brimstone, where the beast and the false prophet are, and shall be tormented day and night for ever and ever" (Rev. 20:10). This is a reference to hell, which is the lake of fire. If you want to argue about its being literal fire, that is all right. It is even more literal than fire and worse than fire. Fire is a very weak symbol of how terrible it is going to be. After all, these are spiritual beings which are mentioned here, and fire as we know it would have no effect upon a spiritual being. Also, we learn from this verse that the Devil is not in hell today. A great many folk think he is there now, but instead he is very busy in your town and mine. Also, he has quite an army of helpers, both supernatural and natural—many folk are helping him, perhaps without realizing it.

Also, the Devil will be responsible for the terrible persecution of believers and especially of Israel during the Great Tribulation of the last days. He will be cast out of heaven: "And the great dragon was cast out, that old serpent, called the Devil, and Satan, which deceiveth the whole world: he was cast out into the earth, and his angels were cast out with him" (Rev. 12:9). Satan will be bound during the kingdom age: "And I saw an angel come down from heaven, having the key of the bottomless pit and a great chain in his hand. And he laid hold on the dragon, that old serpent, which is the Devil, and Satan, and bound him a thousand years, And cast him into the bottomless pit, and shut him up, and set a seal upon him, that he should deceive the nations no more, till the thousand years should be fulfilled: and after that he must be loosed a little season" (Rev. 20:1-3). And finally he will be consigned to the lake of fire, which we have seen in Revelation 20:10.

SODOM AND GOMORRAH SINNED IN SEXUALITY

Even as Sodom and Gomorrha, and the cities about them in like manner, giving themselves over to fornication, and going after strange flesh, are set forth for an example, suffering the vengeance of eternal fire [Jude 7].

This is Jude's third example of apostasy in the past. He has mentioned Israel in their unbelief, the angels which kept not their first estate, and now the people of Sodom and Gomorrah and the cities about them. These cities were so completely judged that they probably are buried beneath the Dead Sea today. Some people believe that they have located them. I am not sure whether or not this is true, and the exact location is unimportant. The important thing to know is that God destroyed these cities because the people defiled their flesh. They were given over to homosexuality or sodomy.

It is interesting that in the parlance of our day sodomy is called homosexuality, adultery is called free love, the drunkard is a respected alcoholic, and the murderer is temporarily insane. Satan is doing a good job of indoctrinating the world with a new vocabulary. Nevertheless, sodomy in God's sight is gross immorality and the vilest sin of all. The fact that God has judged men in the past for sins of sensuality ought to be a warning to our generation. God will judge any civilization that moves too far in this direction, and I wonder if we haven't done just that.

MODERN APOSTATE TEACHERS IDENTIFIED

Likewise also these filthy dreamers defile the flesh, despise dominion, and speak evil of dignities [Jude 8].

These apostate teachers are the ones that we are to beware of. As Jude puts it back in verse 4, they "crept in unaware"; that is, they came in sideways, they came in the side door, they slipped into the church under false colors. Their credentials and their creeds were not the same. They pretended to be something they were not.

There are four points of identification of apostate teachers that Jude gives to us in this verse:

1. They are "filthy dreamers." You will notice that the word *filthy* is in italics in the Authorized Version, which indicates that it is not in the better manuscripts, and we can actually leave it out. They are dreamers—they live in an unreal world, a world that does not exist.

My feeling is that the theological liberal has never dealt with reality. Liberalism is rather romantic. It sounds good on paper. It is nice to be able to solve all your problems by positive thinking, but there is a lot of power in negative thinking also. We need today to learn how to say no as well as to say yes. Liberals are dreamers in the sense that they will not face up to reality.

Many years ago I read an editorial in *Woman's Home Companion* which refers to a group of liberals who have since disappeared from the scene (however, there is a new crop of them abroad in the land today). The editorial reads:

> A pledge "to have no part in any war" has been taken by a large body of leading Protestant clergymen in the east. Among them are some of the wisest and most influential ministers we have— men such as Fosdick, Holmes and Sockman in New York for example. This Covenant of Peace Group declares that war settles no issues, is futile and suicidal and is a denial of God and the teachings of Christ. It asserts that the "chain of evil" which holds us to war can and must be broken now. This is noble doctrine. However much events may lead us to differ with it, when these bold and sincere men stand in their pulpits and preach this rejection of all war, let us remember that these clergymen by their record have earned the right to their belief. In a great democracy suppression of the clergy in war or in peace can never justly become an instrument of policy, as it has under the dictators.

Such antiwar philosophy was carried over recently into the years of the war in Vietnam. It got us into a great deal of trouble and difficulty. The protest meetings that it inspired in this country actually prolonged the war and led to the killing of a great many more American boys who would not have been killed otherwise. Such thinking is to not realize that we live in a big, bad world and that reality is something you have to rub your nose into. It is something that you simply cannot ignore. Even steel-belted tires have to get down and go over the rough places, and some of them go flat, by the way. These men are dreamers. They are dealing with that which is not real at all. As long as we have a big navy and as long as we have atom bombs, it is nice to sit back in the cloister of the church and to make brave statements like this, but it just doesn't work out.

I have a notion that these men stay out of the ghettos and other such places at night, although they may talk very bravely in the daytime. In a denomination which has boasted of how they want to work among the minority groups, they have closed one of their churches which was located in a minority community. I think they have made a big mistake in doing that.

These men are dreamers, and they have gotten into the church and have used the church of the Lord Jesus Christ. Imagine making the statement that war is a denial of the teachings of Christ! The Lord Jesus made the statement, "When a strong man armed keepeth his palace, his goods are in peace" (Luke 11:21). The way you are going to protect your own is by being armed. He also said that the king who is going to war is going to sit down and figure it out (see Luke 14:31). He didn't say it was wrong to figure it out. He said the king had better figure it out, and if he is smart, he will figure out how he is going to carry on that war. May I say to you, these men have failed to face up to what the Lord Jesus Christ really said. He told His disciples, when He first sent them out, that they were to take nothing with them, not even a pocketbook (see Mark 6:7–9). However, when they had returned and He was sending them out to the ends of the earth, He said, "Be sure and take your pocketbook. And you had better take your American Express and Diner's Club cards and your gasoline credit cards. Also, it might be well to have a sword. You will need it to protect yourselves" (see Luke 22:35-36). May I say to you, what nonsense this is—these are dreamers who talk like this. It sounds good to say you don't want to have a part in war. All of us can agree with that. That's sort of like Mother, apple pie, and the American flag—we all are for it. It's great to have no part in war, but we have to face up to reality also. This is a deceptive message that they bring. It's nice to preach it to a well-heeled crowd on Sunday morning when there is no war and everything seems peaceable.

2. The second thing that Jude says about the apostate teachers is

that they "defile the flesh." The thought that Jude has in mind here is that they engage in base and abnormal immorality. This is the same as the "strange flesh" in the cities of Sodom and Gomorrah that he talked about earlier. Many churches today have gone on record that they approve of homosexuality. My friend, God judged the cities of Sodom and Gomorrah. The angels are also a warning to us because they are going to be judged—they are being held for a judgment. And God would not let even His own people whom He had brought out of Egypt enter the Promised Land because of their unbelief. All these are examples to us today, and we had better recognize the fact that God will judge our "new morality." It is neither new morality nor new immorality; there is really nothing new about it. It goes back to Sodom and Gomorrah, and it goes back even to the days of Noah.

3. These apostate teachers "despise dominion," which means they reject authority. They are the crowd that wants to get rid of the death penalty. They are the crowd that wants to turn everybody loose to do his thing in his own way. We are seeing what is taking place as a result. Society has broken out today like a cancer in the body politic. We thought we were a civilized people, but we are nothing in the world but a group of savages. And it is because of this matter of despising dominion, of rejecting authority. We want certain laws repealed. For example, we don't want divorce. The argument given is that there is no reason to have divorce laws, that we ought to just let people stop living together. This breaks right across the morality of any nation, my friend, for the home is the bedrock of any society. During the war in Vietnam, it was tragic to see men with their collars buttoned in the back leading in the protest marches. I felt that the collar buttoned in the back was a real token that they were going in the wrong direction.

4. False teachers "speak evil of dignities." This means that they disrespect dignities. They protest against rules and those in authority. In other words, they take it out on the police because they represent authority, or they take it out upon men in high places. The president, the governors, and the mayors are made responsible for anything that happens in the nation or the state or the city, regardless of whether they are responsible or not. Why? Because there has been a loss of respect for authority. Now I will grant you that some men in authority have not

been worthy of respect, but the office certainly demands respect. Jude will give us an example of this in the next verse.

Let's notice again the characteristics of these apostates who have come into the church. They came in the side door. They are ungodly. They turn the grace of God into lasciviousness. They deny the Lord Jesus Christ. They are dreamers, they defile the flesh, they despise dominion, and they have disrespect for dignities. These are the things that characterize them, and they are dangerous because of the way they have come into the church.

For ten long and weary years, the Greeks laid siege to the city of Troy, but they did not make a dent in the fortifications. It seemed impregnable, and they could not get an entrance into the city. Then there came forth a suggestion. The suggestion was to build a wooden horse with soldiers concealed inside, to leave it outside the gate, and then to pretend to sail away. So they made the wooden horse, the soldiers were put inside, and it was put by the gate of the city of Troy. Well, curiosity got the best of the Trojans. When they saw the Greeks sailing away, they thought the war was over. They went out, saw the horse, and decided to pull it inside the city. It certainly was a novelty, something to have. That night, the soldiers who were on the inside climbed out, and they were able to unlock the gates of the city from the inside. In the meantime, under cover of darkness, the fleet of Greek ships returned. They had only pretended to sail away. What an entire army of mighty men could not do from the outside in ten years, a few soldiers did from the inside. In the same way, the church has been harmed today from the inside and has been taken over by liberalism. Actually, the church has never been harmed from the outside. Persecution caused it to grow by leaps and bounds. Today we are witnessing the destruction of the church from the inside—it's an inside job. Christ was betrayed from the inside, not from the outside. One of His own betrayed Him over to His nation; His nation betrayed Him over to the Romans, and the Romans brought Him to the cross. The church is being betrayed today by the ones who have gotten in by the side door.

The apostasy that was a little cloud the size of a man's hand is now a raging storm that is lashing across the church, casting up foam and fury. We need to hang out this epistle as a storm warning because the apostasy is here in our midst today. I do not say this with any joy or bitterness, but I make it as a statement of fact. All the great denominations of the past are largely gone; that is, they have departed from the faith, probably never to return. They've gone into never-never land. As far as I know, there is no record of a church or any organization or an institution, having once departed from the faith, ever returning. I am told there have been some individuals who have, but I do not know any of them.

The Wesley movement which began in England, for example, was a come-out movement. It was begun when the church became cold and indifferent in that day, and the church of Wesley became a warm incubator in which to reproduce life. But I am sorry to say that today in many places it is a deep freeze that preserves the outward form of Wesley but does not have the warmth and the life that was once there.

I must be very frank to say that I do not think that fundamentalism as it is today is the answer. I perceive a real weakness which I think will ultimately undermine even fundamentalism. That weakness is this: fundamentalism has been exact and precise in doctrine, but in many places it has been devoid of ethics and morals. There are no high principles and practices. There has been a moral breakdown outside of contemporary society, and, fortunately, it is mirrored in our conservative churches. I was with a group sometime ago which is a fine group, but they are an illustration of what I mean. They are insistent and even belligerent about doctrine and about separation. But when it was called to their attention that one in their midst was guilty of immorality, they actually defended him! The ethical practices of another individual smelled to high heaven although he called himself a fundamentalist. May I say to you, this group took a ho-hum attitude. This hurts the cause of Christ a great deal because it comes from the inside.

We are living in days of apostasy. It may be that there are some who would say to me, "Preacher, you are really being sensational. Aren't you exaggerating just a little bit?" I don't think I am, my friend; in fact, I am not sure but what I am giving this in low key to you. I would like to pass on to you the results of a study that was made and some statements made by liberal preachers some years ago now. The situation today is even more alarming than this:

> Out of a poll of 700 preachers, the following results were given: 48% denied the complete inspiration of the Bible; 24% rejected the atonement; 12% rejected the resurrection of the body; 27% did not believe that Christ will return to judge the quick and the dead. A Washington, D.C., minister said, "We liberal clergymen are no longer interested in the fundamentalist-modernist controversy. We do not believe we should even waste our time engaging in it. So far as we are concerned, it makes no difference whether Christ was born of a virgin or not. We don't even bother to form an opinion on the subject." An Arlington, Va. minister said, "We have closed our minds to such trivial consideration as the question of the resurrection of Christ. If you fundamentalists wish to believe that nonsense we have no objection, but we have more important things to preach than the presence or absence of an empty tomb 20 centuries ago." A leading minister in Washington, D.C., said flatly, "In our denomination what you call the 'faith of our Fathers' is approaching total extinction. Of course a few of the older ministers still cling to the Bible. But among the younger men, the real leaders of our denomination today, I do not know of a single one who believes in Christ, or any of the things that you classify as fundamentals."

My friend, have I exaggerated? Have I overstated the case of whether we are in the apostasy or not?

> **Yet Michael the archangel, when contending with the devil he disputed about the body of Moses, durst not bring against him a railing accusation, but said, The Lord rebuke thee [Jude 9].**

This is a most remarkable verse of Scripture. Here is Wuest's very fine translation of it: "Yet Michael, the archangel, when disputing with the devil, arguing concerning the body of Moses, dared not bring a sentence that would impugn his dignity, but said, May the Lord rebuke you."

Satan is a fallen creature and an avowed enemy of God, yet Michael, when contending about the body of Moses, would not bring a sentence that would impugn the dignity of Satan. Michael even respected the position of Satan. Clement, one of the early church fathers, quotes from an apocryphal writing dealing with the funeral of Moses. When Michael was commissioned to bury Moses, Satan opposed it on the grounds that, since he was the master of the material and matter, the body belonged to him. Michael's only answer was, "The Lord (that is, the Creator) rebuke thee." Satan also brought the charge of murder against Moses. Also it is suggested that Satan wanted to hinder the later appearance of Moses at the Mount of Transfiguration.

Lucifer was a creation of God and apparently the highest creature that God created. And then evil was found in him. Don't think that evil means that he went out and stole something. The evil that was in him was that he put his will against the will of God. He was lifted up by pride, and he wanted to become independent of God. He actually thought he could dethrone God—at least from part of His universe. As far as this world is concerned, God has permitted him to carry on this rebellion, and God has a high and holy purpose in it. But this creature still believes he will be able to take a segment of God's created universe and be the ruler over it. I'm sure that Satan wants this earth as his.

"Yet Michael . . . durst not bring against him a railing accusation, but said, The Lord rebuke thee." Michael didn't curse Satan. He didn't call him a long list of names. I'm sure that many of us would have been perfectly willing to have done that. We really would have read the riot act to him, but Michael didn't. Do you know why? Michael is an archangel, and all he did was to say, "The Lord rebuke you." He didn't go into a long tirade of epithets or of condemnation, although he could have. Why? Michael had respect unto his office, his position—Lucifer had been created the highest creature.

This is a lesson that you and I need to learn. A great many believers have not learned to bow even to God. My friend, you and I are creatures; He is the Creator. What right have you and I to question anything that He does? Don't misunderstand me. If you think that I piously accept everything that comes my way, you are wrong. I talk back to Him many times, and I want to know why He lets certain things happen to me. Maybe you do that also. But we need to recognize that God is the Creator; He is also our Redeemer. He is the One who loves us. But our God is high, holy, and lifted up. He is a just and righteous God. He never makes any mistakes. He never does anything wrong. Everything He does is right and, therefore, you and I can trust Him. But do we do that? Do we respect His authority? Do we respect His person? In that day when men must give an account, the Lord Jesus Christ is going to say, "You said, 'Lord, Lord,' but you didn't do the things I commanded. Each one went his own way and did that which was right in his own eyes." This is the picture of mankind. How about you? How about me today? What a lesson Michael the archangel is to us!

But these speak evil of those things which they know not: but what they know naturally, as brute beasts, in those things they corrupt themselves [Jude 10].

I would like, as best I can, to make this verse understandable to you because it is another very important verse in this epistle. When Jude says, "But these speak evil," the Greek word is *btasphemeō* which by transliteration is our English word *blaspheme*. The apostates actually blaspheme.

"These speak evil of [blaspheme] those things which they know not: but what they know naturally." Jude uses two different words here which are both translated "know." May I say, without recognizing that, it is difficult to determine exactly what Jude means here. The first "know" is *eidō* which speaks of "mental comprehension and knowledge . . . referring to the whole range of invisible things," as Vincent defines it. Knowledge is not confined to what you can pour into a test tube or look at under a microscope, although a great many people think that it is. The finer things of life are things you cannot put under the microscope; you cannot pour them into a test tube. For example, what about a wonderful piece of music? What happens if you try to stick it down a test tube or look at it under a microscope? Music needs to be translated into sound, and the ear needs to hear it—you cannot see it at all; it is actually invisible. Love is also invisible—you couldn't put love under the microscope. How about faith?—you can't put it under the microscope. My friend, there are a great many things I know, and I know them without any proof from the laboratory. I know them because I have experienced them. The Holy Spirit has made them real to my own heart. "But these speak evil of those things which they know not." That Washington, D.C., preacher thought he was very brilliant to say that he no longer believed in the Resurrection. May I say to you, there are many things he doesn't know.

The second word for "know" which Jude uses here is *epistamai*, which means "to understand." Vincent says that it was used "originally of *skill in handicraft*" and that it "refers to palpable things; objects of sense; the circumstances of sensual enjoyment." These are things you can pour into the test tube. All that these folk know is what they can handle and what they can see. They are like brute beasts because, after all, a brute only knows about the hay or the grass or the corn or another animal that it can eat. This refers to that which they know by instinct. For example, in the fall of the year, the ducks are in Canada, having had a nice summer up there, but all of a sudden they take off. Somebody says, "Boy, are they smart! Those ducks know that before long it will be winter, that snow will be on the ground, and that the lake is going to freeze over. So they take off for the south, and they go all the way down to Mexico and into Central America. They are really very smart!" No, they are not. They move just like a beast, just like a bird moves—by instinct. There is no comprehension, no understanding.

This generation that thinks it is so smart because it only believes what it can pour into a test tube is a poor generation. They do not understand anything that a brute beast couldn't understand. They have not reached the higher plane of knowledge, what Paul called *epignōsis*. Paul says, "You *can* know that the Bible is the Word of God. You *can* know that Jesus is the Savior of the world." These men, knowing just physical things, think they know everything that can be known, and they corrupt themselves in these things. This is the picture of the apostates that Jude gives to us.

CAIN, BALAAM, AND KORAH—EXAMPLES
OF APOSTATES

Woe unto them! for they have gone in the way of Cain, and ran greedily after the error of Balaam for reward, and perished in the gainsaying of Core [Jude 11].

Jude has already given three examples of apostate groups: the children of Israel, the angels who rebelled, and the cities of Sodom and Gomorrah. Now we are given another three by way of illustration, and these three are individuals.

"Woe unto them!" The word for "woe" is the Greek word *ouai*. The very pronunciation of this word is a wail—"*Ouai, ouai!*" It denotes a wail of grief or of denunciation. Here it is more a wail of denunciation, but it is both. Of these apostates whom Jude has just identified, he now says, "Woe unto them!"

"For they have gone in the way of Cain." Cain was a religious man but a natural man. He believed in God and believed in religion, but he did it after his own will. He denied that he was a sinner, rejected redemption by blood, and thought that he could come his own way to God. Hebrews 11:4 certainly tells the story: "By faith Abel offered unto God a more excellent sacrifice than Cain, by which he obtained witness that he was righteous, God testifying of his gifts: and by it he being dead yet speaketh." Cain is dead also, yet he speaks. The way of Cain is the way of a man who refused to bring a little lamb which pointed to Christ. In other words, Cain did not come to God by faith. He did not believe God when He said that man was to bring a little lamb for a sacrifice, that without shedding of blood there is no forgiveness of sins, and that the penalty must be paid. Cain thought that he could come to God his own way, and that is the picture of the apostate today. The apostate calls himself a liberal and a modernist; but, my friend, this is as old as the Garden of Eden. Right outside the Garden of Eden, Cain was a modernist and a liberal. He believed in religion and God, but he did it his own way, not God's way.

"And ran greedily after the error of Balaam for reward." Here we have the error of Balaam; in 2 Peter 2:15 it is the *way* of Balaam; and in Revelation 2:14 it is the *doctrine* of Balaam.

In 2 Peter we see the thing that was the undermining of the man; that is, Balaam was guilty of covetousness which is idolatry. He was a hired preacher. He wanted to make a buck with the gift he had, a gift that was apparently God-given. This was the way of Balaam, and it was his undoing. A man can seek for something other than money, however. He can seek for prominence, for popularity, for fame, for applause, or for position. There are many different things which would put a man in the way of Balaam. Jude says that this marks the apostate.

In the Book of Revelation, you have the doctrine of Balaam. Numbers 22–25 tells us that this man could not bring a curse against the nation Israel, and so he told Balak that by sending the Moabite women into the camp of Israel, he would be able to bring fornication and idolatry into their homes through mixed marriages. You can be sure of one thing: from Genesis to Revelation, God warns against the intermarriage of believers and unbelievers. You cannot condone such marriages on any basis whatsoever. It is unfortunate that too many young people are not warned of this because it has resulted in a great deal of unhappiness.

The error of Balaam here in Jude is that he thought God would have to punish Israel for their sins. He did not recognize that there is a morality that is above natural morality. He thought that a righteous God *had* to curse Israel. He was totally unaware of the morality of the Cross. It is taught in the Old Testament that God can maintain and does enforce His authority, but He can be just and the justifier of a believing sinner. Balaam did not understand that God would forgive the nation Israel when they turned to Him. It is sometimes difficult for someone to understand how a man can be converted. When I worked in a bank, was led to Christ, and wanted to study for the ministry, my fellow workers, most of whom were church members, could not understand how I could study for the ministry. And they had ample reason to wonder about that, by the way. They couldn't understand that God had forgiven me and that I had a new life now. They just didn't believe that. They didn't believe it because they couldn't understand it. This is the same problem that Balaam had.

"And perished in the gainsaying of Core [Korah]." You will perhaps recall that Korah led a rebellion against Moses (see Num. 16). He came to the conclusion that Moses was not the only one around who had access to God. Korah rebelled against God's constituted authority, who was Moses. He wanted to intrude into that which was sacred. In effect he asked, "Has God only spoken to Moses? Who does Moses think he is?" Actually, Moses didn't think too much of himself or that he had any undue qualifications; in fact, Moses wanted to disqualify himself as the leader of the people out of Egypt. But God had called Moses, and this man Korah rebelled against him. He contradicted the authority of Moses; he intruded into the office of the priests, and he died. In other words, he was a rebellious man, rebelling against God. Jude says that such rebellion characterizes the apostate.

Notice that the things which are true of these three individuals from the Old Testament are also the things which are true of apostates. Cain did not believe that you need to come to God by faith and that you need a bloody sacrifice because man is a sinner. He believed that if you have a religion, that is all you need. The apostate goes along with that. The error of Balaam is to think that a holy God must punish sin and that sinners cannot be forgiven. The apostate makes the same mistake. He says, "How in the world can the sacrifice of Christ save anyone? A man has to do this for himself." And the apostate rebels against God as Korah did. They assume an authority that is not theirs. They stand in the pulpit and give out politics instead of giving out the Word of God. Instead of telling what God says, they tell people what they say and what they think. A man said to me sometime ago, "I have dropped out of my church. I am tired of listening to a preacher who gives political economics and attempts to stand in the position of being an authority on government. He assumes that he has all knowledge, and he never uses the Word of God. He never tells what God says or what God thinks, and I'm tired of listening to him." I know nothing about that man's church, but I assume that that preacher is an apostate because he has the mark of the apostate. These three men from the Old Testament illustrate this to us today.

MODERN APOSTATE TEACHERS DESCRIBED

In the next few verses the modern apostate teachers are defined and described. You will not find anywhere language more vivid, more graphic, more dramatic, more frightening than the description of the apostate in the last days.

> **These are spots in your feasts of charity, when they feast with you, feeding themselves without fear: clouds they are without water, carried about of winds; trees whose fruit withereth, without fruit, twice dead, plucked up by the roots [Jude 12].**

Again let me share with you Dr. Wuest's translation, which makes the description of the apostate teachers even more vivid:

> These are the hidden rocks in your love feasts, sumptuously feasting with you without fear, as shepherds leading themselves to pasture, waterless clouds carried past by winds, autumn trees without fruit, having died twice, rooted up.

What a picture we have here!

"These are spots in your feasts of charity." The word *spots* is better translated "hidden rocks" by Dr. Wuest. The picture is of hidden rocks which wreck a ship. They make what Paul calls "shipwreck" of the faith, and Paul names two men who evidently ran into an apostate, a hidden rock, and made shipwreck of the faith (see 1 Tim. 1:19–20). An apostate may be compared to the tip of an iceberg. Very little of it is visible, but if a ship runs into it, the ship will go to the bottom of the sea. Oh, how many people there are, especially young people, whose faith has not only been shaken but wrecked by a person who is an apostate!

"These are spots in your feasts of charity." The "feasts of charity" were love feasts which were held in the early church before the communion service. It was a time of fellowship when believers brought food and shared a meal together. The poor could bring very little, but it was a time of sharing what they had. Well, the apostates came in with ravenous appetites. They could eat more than anyone else—"feeding themselves without fear." They were shepherds who were feeding themselves instead of their flock. Not only in the matter of food but also in their failure to teach the Word of God to their flock, it was evident that they were concerned only about themselves.

Milton describes this kind of situation when he writes of his friend, Lycidas. In his poem, he expresses his grief for the young man who had been a great preacher and expositor of the Word but was drowned in the Irish Channel. Milton describes the situation in England as it prevailed in his day: "The hungry sheep look up and are not fed." What a picture of an apostate in the pulpit!

"Clouds they are without water." They may look as if they are filled with the Word of God, but they are empty and dry. They may wear robes and speak in pompous, pontifical voices with great authority. They have had courses in public speaking and homiletics, and they know how to spiritualize a text of Scripture and make it mean something entirely different from what God intended. They are like beautiful clouds that drift across the sky without giving any refreshment to the earth.

In my boyhood days I can remember chopping cotton in the summertime and watching the clouds pass over. Oh, how I prayed for rain so I could quit chopping cotton, but there was no rain in those clouds. They were nothing but snowy white puffs. There was no water in them at all. Well, that is Jude's picture of apostates. They do not have the water of life. They actually know nothing about the Word of God.

"Trees whose fruit withereth, without fruit, twice dead, plucked up by the roots." When the Lord Jesus gave the warning against false teachers, He said, ". . . by their fruits ye shall know them" (Matt. 7:20). Jude says that the apostate has withered fruit, he is "twice dead, plucked up by the roots." It was Dwight L. Moody who said that when a man is born once, he will have to die twice and that when a man is born twice, he will have to die only once. Well, Jude says that the apostates are spiritually dead, dead in trespasses and sins—and yet trying to lead others! Also the apostate's body will have to die; so he is twice dead. What a picture of the apostate—and Jude is not through with him.

> **Raging waves of the sea, foaming out their own shame; wandering stars, to whom is reserved the blackness of darkness for ever [Jude 13].**

In the previous verse he said they were like clouds carried about by the wind. These men generally speak on current events every Sunday. They pick up something out of the newspaper or something they have seen on television, and that becomes their subject for the coming Lord's Day. They do not really give the interpretation of the Word of God which would be applicable for the day.

Now here Jude says that they are "raging waves of the sea." They just stand in the pulpit and rant. Dr. Thayer says that these false teachers are "impelled by their restless passions. They unblushingly exhibit in word and deed, their base and abandoned spirit."

"Wandering stars." Wandering stars just wander through space. They are lawless in that they follow no course whatsoever.

"To whom is reserved the blackness of darkness for ever." This refers to hell. One symbol of hell is fire, and the other is blackness of darkness. The great emphasis has been placed upon the symbol of fire. Hell is literal, of course, but to say it is literal fire isn't quite adequate for this reason: there will be spiritual creatures there as well as man— and the worst sins of man are spiritual sins such as unbelief. Therefore, physical punishment wouldn't be quite adequate. My feeling is that man will wish it were literal fire because it will be so much worse than fire. The other symbol, "blackness of darkness," is to me far more frightening. And I believe that a lost man carries his darkness with him—not only physical darkness but spiritual darkness. John Milton, who had an insight into many spiritual truths, penned these lines:

> He that has light within his own clear breast,
> May sit in the centre, and enjoy bright day;
> But he that hides a dark soul, and foul thoughts

Benighted walks under the midday sun;
Himself is his own dungeon.

That is tremendous! My feeling is that the horrors of hell will be increased by those who go there. For instance, there is a place on earth called Hell's Kitchen. Is the difference in the kind of real estate that is there? No, the difference is in the *people* who are there. This, together with the concept of physical darkness, is to me frightful beyond words. If you have ever been down in Carlsbad Caverns when the lights are turned out, you know what real darkness is. I'd hate to be down there forever, my friend!

We come now to another remarkable passage of Scripture, and the only place it occurs in the Word of God is here in Jude.

And Enoch also, the seventh from Adam, prophesied of these, saying, Behold, the Lord cometh with ten thousands of his saints,

To execute judgment upon all, and to convince all that are ungodly among them of all their ungodly deeds which they have ungodly committed, and of all their hard speeches which ungodly sinners have spoken against him [Jude 14–15].

This prophecy of Enoch is not found in the Old Testament. In Genesis 5 we have the record of Enoch, but we are told nothing about his prophecy. Enoch is not a common name; so we may be sure that the man Jude mentions is Enoch of the antediluvian period, the man who walked with God and God took him.

Now let me quote what Dr. Wuest has written about this Book of Enoch:

The quotation is from the apocryphal Book of Enoch. This book, known to the Church Fathers of the second century, lost for some centuries with the exception of a few fragments, was found in its entirety in a copy of the Ethiopic Bible in 1773 by

Bruce. It consists of revelations purporting to have been given to Enoch and Noah. Its object is to vindicate the ways of divine providence, to set forth the retribution reserved for sinners, and so show that the world is under the immediate government of God.

Enoch prophesied regarding the false teachers of the last days, and that is a remarkable thing! God apparently did not want the Book of Enoch in the canon of Scripture or it would be there—you may be sure of that. Godly men recognized that it was an apocryphal book, but here is one prophecy that God wanted put into His holy Word. It is a prophecy concerning the coming of Christ with His saints.

We know from the record in Genesis that Enoch was translated, that is, he was removed from the earth without dying. And sometime in the future, the church, meaning true believers, is to be removed from the earth without dying. Of course, through the centuries since the time of Christ, believers have been dying so that at the present time most of the church has already passed through the doorway of death. And at the time of the Rapture they are to be caught up together with the living believers to meet the Lord in the air. This teaching is not in the Old Testament at all, yet Enoch is a type or a representative of the believers who will take part in the Rapture. Enoch was removed from the earthly scene before the judgment of the Flood came upon the earth. And the believers who compose the true church will be removed from this earth, will be caught up to meet the Lord in the air, before the judgment of the Great Tribulation breaks upon the earth.

Now, after the Great Tribulation, the Lord Jesus will return to the earth. However, at the time of the Rapture He does not come to the earth, but the believers are caught up to meet Him in the air. When we say that the Rapture is the second coming of Christ, we are not quite accurate if we mean that Christ is coming to earth at that time. No, the Rapture is the removal of the church. Then the visible church which is left on the earth, composed of folk who are not true believers, will totally depart from the faith and will enter the Great Tribulation Period. And at the end of the Tribulation, the Lord Jesus will actually come to the earth "to execute judgment upon all, and to convince all that are ungodly among them of all their ungodly deeds which they have ungodly committed," as Jude has prophesied. This is a remarkable passage of Scripture.

Now notice the penetrating truth brought out in Dr. Wuest's translation of Jude 14–15:

> And there prophesied also with respect to these, the seventh from Adam, Enoch, saying, Behold, there comes the Lord with His holy myriads, to execute judgment against all and to convict all those who are destitute of a reverential awe towards God, concerning all their works of impiety which they impiously performed and concerning all the harsh things which impious sinners spoke against Him.

It is quite interesting that "holy myriads," which has to do with the numbers of the saints, can be supernatural or natural creatures, which probably means that the church will come back with Christ when He returns to the earth. If the church does come back with Him to reign on the earth, obviously it had to leave the earth sometime before. You simply have to believe in the Rapture if you believe that Christ is coming back to earth with His saints.

"To execute judgment upon all." When Christ returns to the earth, He is going to execute judgment. Jesus Himself said this in His Olivet Discourse. It is mentioned again and again in the Word of God, and we have seen it in the Old Testament.

"To convince all that are ungodly among them" or, as Dr. Wuest has translated it, "to convict all those who are destitute of a reverential awe towards God." They are ungodly in the sense that they leave God out. And that is something that is quite popular today.

"Of all their ungodly deeds which they have ungodly committed." Dr. Wuest translates it: "concerning all their works of impiety which they impiously performed." Their works are actually anti-God.

"And of all their hard speeches [harsh things] which ungodly sinners have spoken against him."

Now this prophecy of Enoch, and it is a great prophecy, deals with the judgment upon the organized church which will be in total apostasy after the Rapture. You see, the Rapture will rupture the church—the true believers will leave the earth, and the makebelievers will remain and will be here when Christ comes to judge men in that day.

> **These are murmurers, complainers, walking after their own lusts; and their mouth speaketh great swelling words, having men's persons in admiration because of advantage [Jude 16].**

Here are five additional identifications of apostates. (1) They are murmurers. Murmuring means to mutter complaints. This is not loud, outspoken dissatisfaction but muttering against God in an undertone. (2) They are complainers, complaining about their lot in life, discontented, never satisfied. If they recognize God at all, they blame Him for everything that has happened to them. I have received hundreds of letters from folk who tell me how discontented, dissatisfied, and unhappy they were with their lot. Then when they came to Christ, all of that changed. And another characteristic of apostates is that (3) they walk after their own lusts or desires. Those desires could be good or bad—not necessarily desires which are base like immorality. It could be anything that leaves God out. It could be a sailing boat, good music, or literature, or even religion in which they find a certain amount of satisfaction, but in their hearts they are discontented. (4) Their mouth speaks great swelling words; that is, they are immoderate and arrogant; they use extravagant language, which is fizz and foam but has no content. I was rather amused by listening to a politician being interviewed. He used a great many modern expressions which are being overworked today. When he had finished, I analyzed what he had said and realized that he hadn't said anything—he had been just talking. He had not committed himself to anything whatsoever. Well, there are a great many men in the ministry who talk like that also. (5) They have men's persons in admiration because of advantage. This is literally "admiring countenances." They are great at applauding others—and they say a lot of things which are not true—because they are looking to men for their promotion, their advantage. You may recall that the Epistle of James has something to say about this: "My brethren, have not the faith of our Lord Jesus Christ, the Lord of glory, with respect of persons. For if there come unto your assembly a man with a gold ring, in goodly apparel, and there come in also a poor man in vile raiment; And ye have respect to him that weareth the gay clothing, and say unto him, Sit thou here in a good place; and say to the poor, Stand thou there, or sit here under my footstool: Are ye not then partial in yourselves, and are become judges of evil thoughts?" (James 2:1–4).

We see this kind of thing going on in our churches all the time. I went into a church sometime ago where I was to preach. The folk didn't know me very well—certainly the ushers did not. Since I arrived early, I thought I would just go in without identifying myself. When I entered the sanctuary, two ushers were busy talking to each other and paid no attention to me; so I just waited. Finally one of them said, "Want a bulletin?"

"Yes, thank you."

"Where do you want to sit?"

"Well, I don't know. Where would you want to seat me?"

"How about taking that seat right there." He wasn't about to take me down to the front section although there were plenty of seats available. He was not in a friendly mood at all. So, instead of sitting down, I just walked on back. Later when I came out on the platform, I looked back at that usher. Believe me, he was white. After the service he came to me very apologetically. He said, "I didn't know you were going to be our speaker today. I didn't realize that you were Dr. McGee."

"Well," I said, "it really wasn't very important for you to recognize me because, very frankly, I was going to preach here today regardless of whether the ushers let me in or not. But I really think it is important that you usher strangers and visitors to a seat and be very friendly with them."

My friend, as believers we certainly should not have "men's persons in admiration because of advantage." Yet I notice this attitude both in churches and in certain Christian schools. One school will give a man from another school an honorary doctor's degree— something he didn't work for. Then that brother will arrange to have his school confer a doctor's degree on the brother who gave him his degree.

Also, this same type of thing is sometimes practiced by preachers. We speak in a certain church, and the pastor introduces us as some great person, which we certainly are not. Then when he comes over to our church to speak, we introduce him as some great person—whether he is or not. Frankly, we should not use that method because it is less than honest. And that is the method of apostates. They do not look to God. They are not concerned whether or not the Lord Jesus will say to them, "Well done, thou good and faithful servant." They are more concerned to have the applause of the crowd.

When I was in a certain conference, a very timid preacher came to me with a question. He asked, "Do you preach in your church the way you are speaking here?"

"Certainly. Why not?"

"Well, if I preached that way in my church, I am confident that I would have to resign."

I said to him very frankly, "I certainly feel sorry for you, and I think that your church is in a bad way. The message you heard me give was given in my church before I came here—I practiced on them!"

Having men's persons in admiration because of some advantage they will get from it, looking to men for promotion instead of looking to God for promotion, is certainly a condemnation and the mark of an apostate.

OCCUPATION OF BELIEVERS IN DAYS
OF APOSTASY

In verses 17–19, believers are warned by the apostles that these apostates would come. Then in verses 20–25, we will see what believers must do in these days of apostasy.

BELIEVERS WARNED THAT APOSTATES
WOULD COME

Jude reminds believers that the apostles warned that these apostates would come. In other words, he is saying that this ought not to disturb us. The apostasy is something God has permitted, and He has permitted it for a purpose.

But, beloved, remember ye the words which were spoken before of the apostles of our Lord Jesus Christ [Jude 17].

Jude is turning away from describing the apostates, and he says, "But, beloved." He is turning the page as it were, and now he is talking to the beloved. The beloved are not those beloved of Jude. (However, I do think Jude loved them because he would not have written such a strong epistle if he had not loved them and desired to tell them the truth.) The word he uses here means that they are beloved of God. These are the ones who are experiencing the love of God in their lives, and for that reason they are called "beloved."

"Remember ye the words which were spoken before of the apostles of our Lord Jesus Christ." All the way through the Word of God, you will find that we are told to remember. In other words, we are to remember the Word of God. You and I should know the Word of God so that our memories can call it up when we need to have these great truths brought to our attention.

"But, beloved, remember ye the words which were spoken before of the apostles of our Lord Jesus Christ." This is evidence that Jude was not the apostle by that name. He is, as we have indicated, Jude, the half brother of the Lord Jesus. In spite of his blood relationship to Jesus, he takes a very humble attitude. He will use the apostles to corroborate what he is going to say, as he has done before in this epistle. He said earlier, "What I am going to write to you about the apostasy is not new with me. I'm not the only one who has written on it. Others have written of it beforehand." Now he says here, "You are to remember the words that were spoken to you by the apostles of the Lord Jesus Christ." We will see before we finish this epistle that it is all-essential to know what the Word of God has to say. I do not believe that you can stand for God in this world without tripping up unless you have a knowledge of the Word of God—it is essential. I have seen individual after individual, both men and women, trip up and fall in their Christian walk. I can attribute every such instance that I know of to a lack of knowledge of the Word of God. How important it is for us to know what the Word of God has to say.

We come now to a very important passage of Scripture where I feel that I need a special anointing of the Holy Spirit as I write because it deals with a distinction that is not always made today.

> **How that they told you there should be mockers in the last time, who should walk after their own ungodly lusts.**

> **These be they who separate themselves, sensual, having not the Spirit [Jude 18–19].**

I will begin by giving you Dr. Wuest's translation of verses 17–19:

> But, as for you, divinely-loved ones, remember the words which were spoken previously by the apostles of our Lord Jesus Christ, that they were saying to you, In the last time there shall be mockers ordering their course of conduct in accordance with their own passionate cravings which are destitute of reverential awe towards God. These are those who cause divisions, egocentric, not holding the spirit.

In verses 17–18, Jude says in effect, "Remember what the apostles said to you. They told you that there would come mockers in the last time and that they would walk after their own ungodly lusts." That is, the desires of the apostates are totally apart from God and from the will of God.

In verse 19 Jude defines the apostates: "These be they who separate themselves, sensual, having not the Spirit." He has given us so many descriptions of the apostate that there is no reason for us to miss him at all. I believe that you can test an unregenerate person, even an unregenerate minister, by the Word of God. I like to say that I use the Word of God as a Geiger counter. When I give out the Word of God, the Geiger counter registers, and I get a response from the folk who have heard it. Many tell us how the Word of God has actually revolutionized their lives and their homes. It has made everything different, even for those who are believers. But there is another group of people who think that I am a loony bird, that I'm way out in left field, and that teaching the Word of God is a very foolish sort of thing. So you can see that the Geiger counter of the Word of God works, and by it you can test the unregenerate person.

"These be they who separate themselves." First of all, Jude says that the apostates cause divisions in the church. Vincent says that Jude is speaking of those who "cause divisions in the church. . . . Of those who draw a *line through* the church and set *off* one part from another." Liberalism was responsible for splitting the great denominations of the church. The liberals took over the church and then said that the fundamentalists were the ones dividing it. Of course, it was not the fundamentalists who divided the church. They were the ones who were holding to the great doctrines upon which the denominations were founded. The original creeds of all the denominations are sound creeds. Although they differ a little at some points, there are no differences at all on the great basics.

The liberals were first called modernists because they wanted to change things. They never liked that name, but they like the name of liberal today. However, the liberal, instead of being broad-minded, whether he is in theology or politics, is to my judgment the most narrow-minded person in the world. Frankly, he is a dangerous man to deal with, because he will deal with you in a vitriolic manner, with bitterness and hatred, and he will not mind hurting you.

"Sensual"—the word is *psuchikos* from which we get our English word *psychology*. It means a life that centers about the individual; that is, the "I." It is an egotistical way of living in which the individual becomes all important: "I come first." It is selfish; it is natural. It is the life of the unrenewed man, the man who is not born again.

This is Alford's statement:

The *psuchē* [that is, the soul] is the centre of the personal being, the "I" of each individual. It is in each man bound to the spirit, man's higher part, and to the body, man's lower part; drawn upwards by the one, downward by the other. He who gives himself up to the lower appetites, is *sarkikos* (fleshly): he who by communion of his *pneuma* (spirit) with God's Spirit is employed in the higher aims of his being, is *pneumatikos* (spiritual). He who rests midway, thinking only of self and self's interests, whether animal or intellectual, is the *psuchikos* (sensual), the selfish man, the man in whom the spirit is sunk and degraded into subordination to the subordinate *psuchē* (soul).

The natural man, the sensual man, is a selfish man who lives like an animal. He wants to get all he can. He wants to eat all he can. He wants to get all the money and favor he can. He lives entirely for himself. All this has to do with a man in his natural makeup today.

"Having not the Spirit." The apostates do not have the Holy Spirit of God; they are not indwelt by the Spirit of God. You will remember that when Paul got to Ephesus, this was the question he directed to those people who were passing as believers but who were not believers. They had heard only of the baptism of John, and Paul asked them, "Did you receive the Holy Spirit when you first believed?" They knew nothing about it. They had heard about the ministry of John but had not been taught about the Lord Jesus' death and resurrection. When Paul explained these things to them, they accepted Christ and received the Holy Spirit (see Acts 19:1–7).

We need to understand that man is a tripartite being; that is, he has a threefold nature. In 1 Thessalonians 5:23 we read: "And the very God of peace sanctify you wholly; and I pray God your whole spirit and soul and body be preserved blameless unto the coming of our Lord Jesus Christ." Man has a body, a soul, and a spirit.

If you read very carefully the account of the creation of man in the Book of Genesis, you will find that physically, man was taken from the ground. There are about fifteen elements in the dirt which are made into our bodies. When we get through with our bodies, at the time of death, we will be moving out of them, and these bodies will return back to the earth. At the resurrection of the believer, the body will be raised a spiritual body. It is sown in corruption, and it is going to be raised in incorruption.

What happened to this physical man that God created? He was given what we would call a soul—but that word is often misunderstood. He was given the psychological part of himself; that is, that part which directs him in his approach to the physical universe. He gets hungry; so he goes and eats. He desires entertainment, and he provides that for himself. He may be a very generous individual, very amiable, very attractive, and he may have what we call charisma. Many unsaved people are like that. They are likable folk, and I sometimes wish that all believers were as gracious as some unsaved people whom I meet. Although unsaved folk can be very attractive on the surface, they are very different underneath, of course. This is man's psychological nature.

But God also breathed into man's breathing places the breath of life, or the wind, the pneuma, the spirit. This is man's human spirit, and it is above the psychological. It is that which looks to God, that which longs for God, that which wants to worship.

Man, therefore, has a tripartite nature. He is a trinity: the body or the physical side, the soul or the psychological side, and the spirit or the pneumatic side. The psychological side is what Jude calls "sensual" here in verse 19.

Now what really happened at the fall of man? I like to think of man in his tripartite nature as a house with three floors. On the first floor is the dining room and the kitchen—that is the physical. On the second floor is the library and the music room—that is the psychological. On the top floor is a chapel, a place to worship—that is the spiritual. On the top floor is also the Word of God, because man will not understand it without the Spirit of God leading him; the natural man would not even want it. The spiritual was on the top floor, but at the Fall, man actually died spiritually, and the house turned upside down. The physical side got up on top. Man today in his natural state is primarily physical. Meat and potatoes are top priority. Self-preservation is the first law of life. Man is like the animal world in that he is physical, but man is also psychological. He is self-conscious. He enjoys music. He loves beauty. And he also indulges in immorality. This is the area, the sensual part of man, that Jude refers to here. At the Fall, therefore, the spiritual part of man died. Man no longer had a capacity for God; in fact, he was now an enemy of God.

However, when you and I came to Christ and trusted Him as Savior, we were given a new nature, and that new nature can now respond to the Holy Spirit of God. But we still have that old nature. We are still fleshly, and we can live in the flesh. Paul had a great deal to say about this in the eighth chapter of Romans. He writes in verse 5: "For they that are after the flesh [this is the natural man, the apostate] do mind the things of the flesh [that is all they are interested in]; but they that are after the Spirit the things of the Spirit [these folk seek to please God]." Paul goes on in verse 6 to say, "For to be carnally minded is death; but to be spiritually minded is life and peace." When you live in the lower nature—the psychological, the sensual—you are dead to God and have no fellowship with Him. That fellowship is broken. John says, "If we say that we have fellowship with him, and walk in darkness, we lie, and do not the truth" (1 John 1:6). But he who lives in the Spirit and attempts to please God is truly living it up. The spirit of such a man, instead of going downward and doing the things the flesh wants to do, does the things God wants done. Now Paul says in Romans 8:7, "Because the carnal mind is enmity against God [this is the reason Adam ran away from God]: for it is not subject to the law of God, neither indeed can be." You cannot bring that old nature into obedience to God. You cannot reform man. Romans 8:8–9 tells us: "So then they that are in the flesh cannot please God. But ye are not in the flesh, but in the Spirit, if so be that [lit., *since*] the Spirit of God dwell in you. . . ." You cannot please God in the flesh. You can only please Him when you yield to Him and come to the place where He can use you.

This brings me to consider what happens when a man is converted. Before our conversions, you and I were dead in trespasses and sins. We could walk around, we were physically alive, but we were spiritually dead. When a man hears the Gospel, the Spirit of God applies it to his heart, and he trusts Christ. We say that he is born again. The spiritual nature is reborn, and he now has a capacity for God. There is no power in that new nature; so the Holy Spirit comes to dwell within him. This is what Paul meant when he wrote, "But ye are not in the flesh, but in the Spirit, if so be that the Spirit of God dwell in you . . ." (Rom. 8:9).

In other words, the indwelling Spirit is the mark that you are a child of God. The Holy Spirit is not something that you get ten days or so after you are converted. If you don't get Him at the moment you are converted, you are not converted because it is the Holy Spirit who regenerates—we are "born of the Spirit" (see John 3:8). The Holy Spirit is there not only to help you but also to interpret to you the Word of God. And the Word of God is no longer foolishness to you, because a new world and a new life have been opened to you.

However, there is the struggle that goes on which Paul talks about in Galatians 5:17: "For the flesh lusteth [warreth] against the Spirit, and the Spirit against the flesh: and these are contrary the one to the other: so that ye cannot do the things that ye would." There are these two natures within a believer. The old nature, this lower nature, this psychological part of man, wants to turn away from God. This spiritual part now wants to turn to God. If you are a child of God, you know about that conflict. There are times when you want to turn away from Him, and there are times when you want to turn to Him. This is the reason most of us are like a roller coaster in our Christian lives. We go up today, and it is great, but then we go down tomorrow. What a trip it is—up and down! It ought not to be that way, but, unfortunately, most of us would have to testify that that is true of us.

In 1 Corinthians 15:45 Paul talks about the Resurrection, and he has this to say: ". . . The first man Adam was made a living soul [that is, the psychological]; the last Adam was made a quickening spirit [that is, a life-giving spirit]." This is the difference between Adam No. 1 and Adam No. 2, between Adam in the Garden of Eden and the Lord Jesus Christ on the cross. The Lord Jesus came to give His life that He might be a life-giving Spirit. Paul goes on to say in verses 46–47: "Howbeit that was not first which is spiritual, but that which is natural [Adam was a psychological being]; and afterward that which is spiritual. The first man is of the earth, earthy: the second man is the Lord from heaven." This, I believe, is the big difference between Adam before his fall and the man today who is regenerated. We are today made sons of God and are given a spiritual nature with a capacity for God. Man's highest nature at the beginning was that God breathed into his breathing places, but that was a spirit that could fall. We have a nature today that is a sinful nature, and we will have it as long as we are in this body because it actually controls this body—this is the psychological part of man. But at the moment of regeneration we were given a new nature which responds to God and cannot fall.

When I first studied psychology (it was one of my major areas of study at one time), they said that psychology was the study of the soul of man. Then they got away from that, and they said it was the study of the mind of man. Behaviorism came along and then Freudianism later on, and they took their theory of man further and farther away from anything psychological or even mental. Man became nothing in the world but a sort of robot or IBM computer. You can press a certain button and always get a certain reaction from him. As a result, the saying went around that psychology first lost its soul, and then it lost its mind. I do not know whether it has recovered it or not!

The thing that I want to emphasize here is that the flesh pulls man down and the Spirit pulls man up. Jude says that these apostates never get into the realm of the Spirit—"having not the Spirit." They are "sensual"; they never get above the psychological state. Therefore, it is very easy to tell whether or not you are a child of God, my friend. Paul lists the works of the flesh in Galatians 5:19–21, and if you are producing those in your life, you are living in the flesh. He then lists the fruit of the Spirit in verses 22–23. If you have those things in your life, you are a child of God. But the apostate does not have those things in his life. He cannot have them because he does not have the Spirit of God.

I have spent a little time with this because I feel it is very important that you and I understand ourselves and why we have all the conflicts and frustrations that we Christians have. We have two natures. The psalmist says that we are "fearfully and wonderfully made" (see Ps. 139:14). Man is a very complicated creature. A man walks this earth today with a body that is taken out of the dirt, but he also has a capacity for God. A man who wants to worship and serve God can become a son of God through faith in Jesus Christ—what a glorious prospect this is!

WHAT BELIEVERS MUST DO IN DAYS
OF APOSTASY

Now having described the apostasy that was coming and the apostates who would come into the church, Jude mentions seven things which believers can do in days like these in which you and I are living.

But ye, beloved, building up yourselves on your most holy faith, praying in the Holy Ghost [Jude 20].

"But ye beloved"—he is talking to believers, those beloved of God. What can we do today?

1. "Building up yourselves on your most holy faith." What does he mean by that? Well, building up yourselves on your most holy faith means that you *study* the Word of God. It is my conviction that since God gave to us sixty-six books, He meant that we are to study all sixty-six of them—not just John 3 or John 14 and other favorite passages. Oh, how many Bible classes go over and over the same books: John, Romans, maybe Ephesians, and they don't miss Revelation. Do not misunderstand me, all those books are very important, but what about the other sixty-two books? Why don't we study *all* of them? My friend, if you are going to build up yourself on your most holy faith, you must have the total Word of God. You cannot build a house without a foundation; then you will need to put up some timbers that will hold the roof; then you are going to need a roof on it and siding and plaster on the inside. And this is what the total Word of God will do for you. This is what we are to do in days of apostasy.

Both Peter and Paul urged believers to study the Word of God in days like these. Paul wrote in his swan song: "Study to shew thyself approved unto God, a workman that needeth not to be ashamed . . ." (2 Tim. 2:15). Then in the next chapter Paul said that *all* Scripture is given by inspiration of God. My friend, the recourse that you and I have as children of God in these days is the Word of God.

The reason many folk fall by the wayside is because the seed (which is the Word of God) fell among stones. It didn't get deeply rooted. Unless you study all of the Word of God, get down in the good, rich soil, you are not going to become a sturdy, healthy plant. It won't be long until you will be stepped on and the sun will burn you out. You will not be able to stand in days like these.

Peter in his second epistle, writing of the apostasy, says, "We have also a more sure word of prophecy; whereunto ye do well that ye take heed, as unto a light that shineth in a dark place, until the day dawn, and the day star arise in your hearts: Knowing this first, that no prophecy of the scripture is of any private interpretation" (2 Pet. 1:19-20). You cannot just pull out one or two little verses and think you have a good knowledge of the Bible. It is a tragedy to build a system of doctrine based on a few isolated verses drawn out of the Scriptures.

This reminds me of the story of President Lincoln having his portrait painted. The artist kept shifting Lincoln around trying to get him at an angle so the wart on his face wouldn't show. Finally, after he had him adjusted to his satisfaction, he said, "Mr. Lincoln, how do you want me to paint you?" Lincoln said, "Paint me just as I am—wart and all."

My friend, certainly there are parts of the Word of God that you will not enjoy reading. There are sections that will step on your toes, and you would like to avoid that. But today it is necessary to build up ourselves on our most holy faith because these are days of apostasy.

"Your most holy faith" does not refer to your own personal faith. Rather, it is *the* faith, the body of truth which has been given to us in the Word of God. When the church first came into existence, this was called the apostles' doctrine. Of this Mayor says:

> The faith here is called 'most holy' because it comes to us from God, and reveals God to us, and because it is by its means that man is made righteous, and enabled to overcome the world.

2. "Praying in the Holy Ghost." Jude mentions the second thing we are to do in days of apostasy. The word *Ghost* is the Greek *pneuma*, more frequently translated "Spirit." "Praying in the Holy Spirit" is an unusual phrase, occurring at only one other place in the Scriptures. In the Epistle to the Ephesians, Paul mentions putting on the whole armor of God, and each piece of armor is for defense with the exception

of two items. One offensive weapon is "Praying always with all prayer and supplication in the Spirit, and watching thereunto with all perseverance and supplication for all saints" (Eph. 6:18). The second offensive weapon was mentioned in verse 17, "the sword of the Spirit, which is the word of God." This is precisely what Jude writes. First, we are to build up ourselves on our most holy faith; then we need to pray in the Spirit.

Many years ago in Dallas, Texas, there was a very fine man, Mr. Will Hawkins, who had a radio program which he called "The Radio Revival." I do not know of any program during the depression and afterwards that influenced people more than his program did. One of the features of his radio broadcast was what he called a sword drill, a test of the knowledge of the Word of God, and I thought it was about the best way it could be used. My friend, you and I need a sword drill; that is, we need to listen to God first before He has to listen to us, because we could say a lot of foolish things. We are to take the sword of the Spirit, because we need to build up ourselves in the faith—we should learn to use that sword.

Praying in the Holy Spirit is a little different from handing God a grocery list of "Gimme, gimme, gimme." Don't misunderstand me, petition, as it is called in theology, is a part of prayer. But how about praise and how about worship? Our prayer should include adoration and praise to almighty God. Dr. Earl Radmacher once told me about directing a prayer meeting in a church he pastored. The prayer meetings had been pretty dead, as most church prayer meetings are, unfortunately. They should be the real powerhouse of the church body, but they usually are not. One night Dr. Radmacher announced that they were not going to have any requests but only praise and thanksgiving to God for what He had done for them. Dr. Radmacher said that it turned out to be the briefest prayer meeting they had ever had! It is amazing how few things we thank God for and how little praise goes up to Him. However, petition is certainly important, and prayer that includes that is a real ministry. When Paul asked the Christians in Rome to pray for him, he wrote: "Now I beseech you, brethren, for the Lord Jesus Christ's sake, and for the love of the Spirit, that ye strive together with me in your prayers to God for me" (Rom. 15:30). The word for "strive" is *agonize*. We are to pray like that.

Praying in the Holy Spirit means that we pray by means of the Holy Spirit; we are dependent upon Him. Paul wrote in Romans 8:26, "Likewise the Spirit also helpeth our infirmities: for we know not what we should pray for as we ought: but the Spirit itself maketh intercession for us with groanings which cannot be uttered." You and I actually do not know what to pray for. We are like little children. When I take my little grandson to the store, he wants everything he sees. He asks for things that he shouldn't even have because they would not be good for him. Then I think, *That's just the way we pray.* We are like little children: "Lord, I want this—Lord, give me that." God doesn't always give us what we want. Why doesn't He? Because when we pray like that, we are not praying in the Spirit. We need to learn to let the Holy Spirit make intercession for us.

Years ago a missionary in Venezuela sent me a little cross on which was printed a definition of prayer: "Prayer is the Holy Spirit speaking in the believer, through Christ, to the Father." That is a very good definition of prayer.

My friend, we need to learn to pray. No wonder the disciples, having heard the Lord Jesus pray and thinking of their own little paltry prayers, said, "Lord, teach us to pray" (see Luke 11:1). Many of us need that, but there is very little instruction today about learning to pray. Yet we need to learn to really pray in these days of apostasy.

Keep yourselves in the love of God, looking for the mercy of our Lord Jesus Christ unto eternal life [Jude 21].

This verse gives us two more things we as believers are to do in days of apostasy.

3. "Keep yourselves in the love of God." We need to recognize that God *loves* the believer. We have seen that Jude addresses the believers as "beloved." Let me repeat—this does not imply that *he* loves them or that they love him but that they are beloved of *God.* Again, let me say that you cannot keep God from loving you, although you can put up an

umbrella or a roof so that you will not feel the wrath of God's love. Jude is saying, "Keep yourselves out there in the sunshine of God's love." Let His love flood your heart and life. This is needed in days of apostasy.

4. "Looking for the mercy of our Lord Jesus Christ unto eternal life." There was a man here in Southern California, a professor in a seminary, whom I had asked to preach in the church I served, and someone questioned that he really believed in the rapture of the church. So I had lunch with him and asked him this specific question: "Do you believe in the imminent coming of Christ?"

"I do."

"On what basis do you believe that He will take the church out? That is, on what grounds do you and I expect to be taken out at the time of the Rapture?"

He said very definitely, "I was saved because God extended mercy to me, and when He takes me out of the world at the time of the Rapture, it still will be by the mercy of God."

That is a good answer, and it cleared up all doubts of his position on the rapture of the church.

My friend, as we have seen, the mercy of God is the fact that God has a concern and care for you today. And He has an abundance—He is rich in mercy. He was so concerned about you that He extended His mercy to you and saved you by His grace.

Notice that Jude says, "Looking for the mercy. " The word *looking* is the Greek word *prosdechomai*, meaning "to expect, to wait for." The Lord Jesus wants us to live in an attitude of expectation for His return. At the time of the Rapture, I am expecting to leave this world, and I hope it will happen during my lifetime. But I will be going out because of His mercy, not because of who I am. If it depended upon who I am, I wouldn't make it.

When I first went to Nashville, Tennessee, there was a very fine Bible class there that had been taught the theory of a partial rapture; that is, that only the super-duper saints would go out at the Rapture. They were a wonderful group of folk, and they supported my ministry in Nashville. I even had the privilege of teaching the class several times. However, in talking with some of them, especially the leaders, they made it clear that they expected to go out at the time of the Rapture because they were the super-duper saints, but I had the feeling that they weren't sure about me. Well, I want them and everyone else to know that when the Lord takes the church out, I'm going along—whether you like it or not—because I am *looking* for that mercy of the Lord Jesus Christ.

Now notice Dr. Wuest's translation of verse 21:

With watchful care keep yourselves within the sphere of God's love, expectantly looking for the mercy of our Lord Jesus Christ resulting in life eternal.

And of some have compassion, making a difference [Jude 22].

5. "Of some have compassion." There is some question among Greek scholars as to the correct translation of this verse. Instead of "making a difference," I prefer the rendering "who are in doubt." There are a great many good, sincere folk today who are in doubt. They do have honest doubts, and we need to be patient with them. Being in the ministry I have had some difficulty in being patient with some folk. I remember a woman who came to our midweek Bible study in a church I served many years ago. Every week for six weeks she came to me with some question. I had the feeling that she was trying to trap me or trick me with her questions, and one night I answered her so sharply that she turned and walked out. The woman who always came with her was a member of my church, and she came to me afterward and said, "Dr. McGee, be patient with her. She is a very brilliant woman. In fact, she is listed in *Who's Who*. But she has been in practically every cult here in Southern California, and she is really mixed up. Now she is trying to find her way out. Will you be patient with her?" Well, knowing her background, of course, I was patient after that and answered her questions the best I could. About three months later she accepted Christ as her Savior. I had a wonderful letter after she had returned to Ohio in which she told how the Lord was leading her.

My friend, we are living in days when there is so much doubt cast upon the Word of God that those who really want to believe it have problems in doing so. We do well to be patient with them—they are honest doubters.

And others save with fear, pulling them out of the fire; hating even the garment spotted by the flesh [Jude 23].

6. "And others save with fear, pulling them out of the fire" refers to sinners whom we consider hopeless. It seems impossible that they will ever be saved. And yet I have seen some of these folk come to know Christ by hearing God's Word by radio. Jude admonishes us not to give them up—"others save with fear, pulling them out of the fire." What a tremendous statement!

In Zechariah 3:2 we read this: "And the LORD said unto Satan, The LORD rebuke thee, O Satan; even the LORD that hath chosen Jerusalem rebuke thee: is not this a brand plucked out of the fire?" When God intended to save Jerusalem, He said, "I am just taking a brand out of the fire." Apparently there is no one who is beyond redemption, if they want to be saved.

7. "Hating even the garment spotted by the flesh." The word *flesh* refers to the psychological part of man, the part of man that can go only so far. It can, for example, appreciate good music, but it cannot be acceptable to God. There have been attempts to come up with the right word for this psychological part of man. The word *soul* is not adequate because it doesn't express what it should. Some call it the *selfish* part of man. That is not a good definition because some psychological people are very generous although they are not Christian. Others speak of it as the *animal,* which is even worse. Although these people generally attempt to satisfy the lower nature, *animal* is not the proper word. Still others call them intellectual, which is the worst one of all. Lange, in his *Commentary on the Holy Scriptures,* attempts to adequately describe these folk:

He is becoming flesh, wholly carnal or animal. If allowed to continue he will become utterly dehumanized, or that worst of all creatures, an animal with a reason, but wholly fleshly in its

ends and exercises, or with a reason which is but the servant of
the flesh, making him worse than the most ferocious wild
beast—a very demon—a brutal nature with a fiend's subtlety
only employed to gratify such brutality. Man has the supernatural, and this makes the awful peril of his state. By losing it, or
rather by its becoming degraded to be a servant instead of a lord,
he falls wholly into nature, where he cannot remain stationary,
like the animal who does not "leave the habitation to which
God first appointed him." The higher being, thus utterly fallen,
must sink into the demonic, where evil becomes his god, if not,
as Milton says, his good.

The fact is that the child of God should hate "even the garment spotted
by the *flesh*." God cannot use anything that the flesh produces. Everything that Vernon McGee does in the flesh is repulsive to God; He
hates it. And we should learn to hate it.

This little Epistle of Jude closes with a glorious benediction.

> **Now unto him that is able to keep you from falling, and
> to present you faultless before the presence of his glory
> with exceeding joy,**
>
> **To the only wise God our Saviour, be glory and majesty,
> dominion and power, both now and ever. Amen [Jude
> 24–25].**

Let me give you a literal translation:

> Now unto him who is able to keep you from stumbling, and to
> present you (make you stand) before the presence of his glory
> blameless with great rejoicing, to the only wise God our Savior,
> through Jesus Christ our Lord, be glory and majesty and might
> and authority, before all time both now and forever. Amen.

If you want to know the place that Jesus Christ should have in your life,
especially in these days of apostasy, here it is in this marvelous benediction.

"Through Jesus Christ our Lord"—He is God. And He is our Lord; He should be the Lord of our lives. Glory should be given to Him. We should glorify Him, tell how great He is, how wonderful He is, how mighty He is and mighty to save. He is majestic, the King of Kings and Lord of Lords. He is mighty—all power is given unto Him in heaven and in earth. This universe has not slipped from under His control. All authority belongs to Him, and whether you like it or not, you are going to bow the knee to Him someday.

In these days of apostasy, God's children need to bring glory to the name of Jesus Christ and to try to hold Him up before a gainsaying world.

BIBLIOGRAPHY
(Recommended for Further Study)

Coder, S. Maxwell. *Jude: The Acts of the Apostates.* Chicago, Illinois: Moody Press, 1958.

Ironside, H. A. *Exposition of the Epistle of Jude.* Neptune, New Jersey: Loizeaux Brothers, n.d.

Kelly, William. *Lectures on the Epistle of Jude.* Denver, Colorado: Wilson Foundation, 1970.

Wolff, Richard. *A Commentary on the Epistle of Jude.* Grand Rapids, Michigan: Zondervan Publishing House, 1960.

Wuest, Kenneth S. *In These Last Days: II Peter, II, III John, and Jude in the Greek New Testament for the English Reader.* Grand Rapids, Michigan: Wm. B. Eerdmans Publishing Co., 1954.